Understanding Motor Skills in Children with Dyspraxia, ADHD, Autism, and Other Learning Disabilities

A Guide to Improving Coordination

Lisa A. Kurtz

Jessica Kingsley Publishers
London and Philadelphia

First published in 2008
by Jessica Kingsley Publishers
116 Pentonville Road
London N1 9JB, UK
and
400 Market Street, Suite 400
Philadelphia, PA 19106, USA

www.jkp.com

Copyright © Lisa A. Kurtz 2008

Library of Congress Cataloging in Publication Data
Kurtz, Lisa A.
 Visual perception problems in children with AD/HD, autism and other learning disabilities : a guide for parents and professionals / Lisa A. Kurtz.-- 1st American pbk. ed.
  p. cm.
 Includes bibliographical references and index.
 ISBN-13: 978-1-84310-826-9 (pbk.)
 ISBN-10: 1-84310-826-7 (pbk.)
 1. Attention-deficit hyperactivity disorder. 2. Autism. 3. Autism in children. I. Title.
 RJ506.H9K87 2006
 616.85'89--dc22

                                                    2005037054

British Library Cataloguing in Publication Data
A CIP catalogue record for this book is available from the British Library

ISBN 978 1 84310 865 8

Printed and bound in the United States
by Thomson-Shore, Inc.

Understanding Motor Skills in Children with Dyspraxia, ADHD, Autism, and Other Learning Disabilities

other books in the same series

Visual Perception Problems in Children with AD/HD, Autism and Other Learning Disabilities
A Guide for Parents and Professionals
Lisa Kurtz
ISBN 978 1 84310 826 9

of related interest

Integrated Yoga
Yoga with a Sensory Integrative Approach
Nicole Cuomo
ISBN 978 1 84310 862 7

Can't Play Won't Play
Simply Sizzling Ideas to get the Ball Rolling for Children with Dyspraxia
Sharon Drew and Elizabeth Atter
ISBN 978 1 84310 601 2

Caged in Chaos
A Dyspraxic Guide to Breaking Free
Victoria Biggs
ISBN 978 1 84310 347 9

Developmental Coordination Disorder
Hints and Tips for the Activities of Daily Living
Morven F. Ball
ISBN 978 1 84310 090 4

Living with Dyspraxia
A Guide for Adults with Developmental Dyspraxia: Revised edition
Mary Colley
Foreword by Victoria Biggs
Introduction by Amanda Kirby
ISBN 978 1 84310 452 0

The Adolescent with Developmental Co-ordination Disorder (DCD)
Amanda Kirby
ISBN 978 1 84310 178 9

Kids in the Syndrome Mix of ADHD, LD, Asperger's, Tourette's, Bipolar, and More!
The one stop guide for parents, teachers, and other professionals
Martin L. Kutscher MD
With a contribution from Tony Attwood
With a contribution from Robert R Wolff MD
ISBN 978 1 84310 810 8 hb
ISBN 978 1 84310 811 5 pb

This book is inspired by the many, many special children who have brought sunshine into my life for more than three decades. Among them: Artie, Breanna, Christian, Dakota, Erik, Frankie, Graeme, Hannah, Iris, Jerome, Katherine, Leah, Max, Noah, Olivia, Payce, Quientan, Richie, Stephanie, Troy, Vincent, Willo, Xander, Yvette, and Zackery. Since I plan to continue working for at least another decade, I should still have time to meet a special child whose name begins with the letter "U!" In the meantime, thanks and extra treats for "Uncle George," my special cat who kept me company during long hours of typing!

CONTENTS

List of Figures and Tables

Figures

Tables

INTRODUCTION

Many childhood developmental disorders such as autism, attention deficit disorder (ADD), and other learning disabilities have characteristic symptoms that include problems with physical coordination. It's not hard to recognize a child who struggles with coordination difficulties. This is the child who may present with a normal appearance in every other way, yet constantly attracts the attention of playmates and adults by dropping everything that is handled, tripping over the smallest of obstacles, and falling frequent victim to a variety of minor "accidents" related to physical awkwardness. He or she may have trouble learning to draw or write, cannot easily button clothes or tie shoes, becomes frustrated when learning new skills, and may unfortunately be teased or victimized by other children for being "different," "careless," or "klutzy." It is common for children with these problems to have low self esteem, for they are expected to compete in a society that places high value on athletics and other physical accomplishments, especially during the early childhood years.

The ability to coordinate body movements varies considerably among individuals, not only in childhood but throughout the adult years. Like other aspects of human performance, the quality of a person's motor coordination depends upon the combined influences of several factors, including the rate of developmental maturation, the person's inherited ability or talent, and his or her motivation to practice and refine these skills. Not surprisingly, children who have well-developed motor skills are likely to demonstrate a high degree of motivation to engage in activities like competitive sports, building with construction toys, or throwing balls at targets, because their success with these activities results in a pleasurable experience. They receive praise and positive attention for their performance, which usually fuels a desire to further practice and challenge these skills. In contrast, children who have less skill may avoid physically challenging activities in favor of more sedentary games and diversions, or may demonstrate aggressiveness or clowning behavior during physical activities as a means to gain attention for their efforts. Many children with coordination difficulties possess talent in other areas of development—such as vocabulary or language use, which may be skillfully used to draw attention away from their relative weaknesses in motor skills.

This book was designed to offer practical advice and reference material for parents, teachers, therapists, and others who care for children with mild to moderate developmental delays affecting motor skills. Although specifically written to address the needs of young children with poor coordination in the presence of otherwise normal development, or that which is associated with certain developmental disorders of childhood including attention deficit hyperactivity disorder (ADHD), dyspraxia or developmental coordination disorder (DCD), specific learning disabilities, autism and pervasive developmental disorder—some of the suggestions may also be helpful for children with more significant developmental problems affecting motor development and control, such as cerebral palsy or mental retardation.

Chapter 1 presents an overview of normal motor developmental milestones as a means for estimating the degree of delay in a given child. It discusses the possible causes of delayed motor development. It should help the reader to decide if there is significant cause for worry, and if professional assessment seems indicated. Chapter 2 suggests when and where to obtain further help when there are significant concerns. It describes the roles of various professionals who might be of assistance, and the kinds of tests and procedures that may be used to evaluate the child. Chapter 3 discusses some of the general principles for helping young children to develop competence in activities that challenge motor skills. It offers general guidance for promoting the right kinds of behavior and attitude in children with poor coordination, as well as discussing the controversial nature of some specific therapy approaches. Chapter 4 presents specific teaching strategies and suggested activities to use for learning basic motor skills including motor planning, bilateral integration, balance, fine motor coordination, oral-motor control, and functional vision skills. Chapter 5 addresses strategies for promoting independence in daily living skills, and Chapter 6 addresses learning to cope with problems in the classroom involving proper seating and positioning, learning to write and to use scissors, and developing organizational skills. Finally, Chapter 7 discusses how to help the child to develop a positive self image as a basis for learning to get along well with other children, and how to cope when being teased or bullied by others. While not intended to be a "cookbook" of solutions for children with clumsiness, these activity guidelines will hopefully serve as a general guide for the home and classroom, as well as a stimulus for discussion between parents, teachers, and therapists.

Several appendices are included, containing a list of tests and assessment tools, a recommended reading list, agencies and organizations that provide advice or technical assistance to parents or professionals, and a list of suppliers of toys and other educational materials useful in working with young children.

Part I

UNDERSTANDING THE NATURE OF MOTOR SKILLS

Chapter 1

THE DEVELOPMENT
OF MOTOR SKILLS

Normal motor development

Because the human nervous system is immature at the time of birth, children are expected to grow and develop continually throughout their childhood years. A number of factors combine to influence each child's rate and quality of motor development. Genetic or inherited traits can greatly impact upon strength, agility, and general talent for physical challenges. For this reason, children born to parents of short stature and a tendency towards obesity may be less likely to become skilled basketball players than children born to tall, athletically built parents. Cultural and lifestyle differences among families also impact upon both the presence of opportunities to engage in challenging physical activity as well as the importance placed on these activities within the unique culture of the family. Children living in rural areas where parents encourage daily hiking, biking, or other healthy outdoor activities may be more motivated to challenge themselves physically than children living in an inner-city environment with parents who favor more sedentary pastimes. We know that, for successful motor learning, the child must receive frequent opportunities to physically explore his or her surroundings in order to develop an appreciation and awareness of the body interacting with the environment. That is why, when we think of very young children, we usually think of them being very active. It is typical for young children to want to run, climb, jump, and to practice balancing on a curbstone or throwing objects at a target. This is the natural way that children learn about their bodies and how they establish mastery over their environment.

The famous developmental psychologist Jean Piaget described the close association between perceptual learning and the development of physical proficiency (Piaget and Inhelder 1969). Early movements made by the very young infant are largely reflexive, or involuntary, in nature. The infant is exposed to a wide variety of perceptual experiences through all of the body's senses. These include vision, hearing, touch, taste, smell, *vestibular* awareness (sense of gravity and motion that comes from receptors located in the vestibular apparatus in the inner ear) and *proprioception* (sense of body position and motion from joint and muscle receptors). Initially, these sensations are experienced passively as the infant is held, rocked, stroked, or fed. Gradually, the infant learns that certain involuntary, reflexive movements can result in pleasurable sensory experiences, and attempts to repeat the motions voluntarily in order to repeat the pleasurable sensation.

For example, very young infants possess a reflexive response called "rooting." When one side of the face is lightly stroked, the infant turns his or her head toward that side. This is the instinctive way that the infant locates food, for the motion frequently results in locating the mother's nipple when the child is held against her breast. This reflexive movement results in a pleasurable experience involving the smell and taste of food, the physical sensations of sucking, and the satisfying feel of a full tummy. In addition, the mother may provide a loving touch, calming stimulation through rocking, soft words of encouragement, and a pleasant smile with eye contact toward the infant. Virtually every sensory system of the body is stimulated in an emotionally positive manner as a result of the infant's simple movement. When reflexive movements are repeated because the infant finds them to be pleasurable or rewarding, movement becomes active, or voluntary. In this way, we might think of motor learning as much as a mind–body process as a function of physical maturation.

Repetition is also an important concept in motor learning. New motor skills must be practiced, or rehearsed, in order to become strong, fluid, and well coordinated. Given enough practice, some movements become so automatic that we are hardly aware of them and need not attend to how well we are executing them. For example, an unexpected sneeze causes most people to automatically, quickly, and accurately bring their hand to their mouth. If the person is right handed, it is usually the right hand that is brought to the mouth, but if the right hand is otherwise engaged, for example stirring a pot of soup, the left hand will execute the motion just as accurately. Children who lack the motivation to learn, who do not enjoy physical challenges, or whose sensory perception results in confusing or unpleasant feedback from movement may not become sufficiently motivated to practice motor skills. As a result, they may show both a delay in developing certain motor skills, and a lack of automaticity, requiring them to think more about their movements than the average child.

For most children, the development of motor skills occurs throughout childhood, and follows certain predictable steps or stages, also known as *developmental milestones.* Most people who are familiar with children can describe at least some typical developmental milestones. For example, everyone knows that an infant must first learn to sit, then to pull up to standing, before finally taking a first step, usually sometime around one year of age. Other developmental motor sequences may be less familiar to those without professional training, but are equally as predictable. For example, when learning to grasp a small object such as a block, the infant first rakes or scratches at the object with the whole hand, then learns to precariously grasp the object with the side of the hand closest to the pinky finger, then with the side of the hand closest to the thumb, until finally, at around one year of age, he or she learns to grasp using the more precise method of opposing the thumb to the index and middle fingers.

We recognize that there is considerable variability in the development of each individual child. For example, on average boys tend to walk a little later than girls, and children born to the same family may learn to walk at different ages. Despite this, there is enough predictability in typical development to understand when and in what order or sequence certain milestones ought to develop. This allows us to identify children whose development is delayed or advanced when compared to other children the same age. For example, we would predict that frequent falling during running is normal for a child of 18 months, but is not normal for a five-year-old child, and that the inability to hold a crayon with the fingers is normal for an infant but not for a school-aged child. Table 1.1 presents an overview of typical developmental milestones in young children, including milestones that relate to the development of motor skills.

When a child's rate of development differs slightly from the norm, there may or may not be cause for concern. However, even slight delays in motor development warrant monitoring.

Delayed or impaired motor development

Many childhood disorders include motor delay or clumsiness as part of the condition. For example, cerebral palsy is a condition occurring in very early childhood that involves damage to the parts of the brain that influence muscle tone and that control movement. Muscle tone is the amount of tension present in the muscles, and helps to prepare the muscles for action. In cerebral palsy, there may be too much tone (spasticity), too little tone (floppiness), or fluctuating tone. Children with cerebral palsy have a variety of difficulties affecting movement, and as a result are frequently very uncoordinated. In contrast, children with mental retardation demonstrate delays in all areas of development, and may appear to be clumsy when compared to other children of the same age. Although they may attain motor

Table 1.1 Milestones of typical development

Age	Fine motor	Gross motor	Speech/language	Cognitive/perceptual	Personal/social
3 months	Hands remain open during rest	Head lags behind when pulled to sitting from lying on back	Coos/smiles in response to pleasant tones Laughs aloud Searches for sound with eyes	When lying on back, promptly looks at toy and follows with eyes	Shows anticipation of bottle/food through facial response
6 months	Passes toy from hand to hand when lying on back Rakes at tiny object using all fingers	Plays with feet while lying on back Rolls in both directions Sits with hands propped forward Stands and bounces when held by both hands	Pays attention to music or singing Understands "hi" and "bye-bye" Imitates familiar sounds, babbles (e.g. "wawa," "baba")	Shakes rattle on purpose	Holds own bottle Drinks from cup that is held by adult Mouths/gums hard cookie or cracker
9 months	Grasps block with fingers, not palm of hand Wrist is extended (bent back) during grasp of block	Head leads when pulled to sitting from lying on back Creeps or crawls on all fours Sits independently with hands free for play Pulls to stand at low table	Stops activity when name is called Understands "no" Uses some gesture language Participates in "pat-a-cake," "peek-a-boo"	Holds one block or toy in each hand and bangs together at midline	Feeds self cracker Finger feeds small bits of food (like cereal or cut-up vegetables)

Age					
12 months	Builds tower of two blocks Uses mature pinch grasp (thumb and tip of forefinger) Holds crayon using fisted grasp Helps to turn pages in a book	Stands alone without support Takes first steps	Responds to simple commands without any gestures Knows one body part Beginning to use single words meaningfully	Imitates scribbling with crayon	Brings pre-filled spoon to mouth, but spills Holds handle of cup while drinking Holds out arms and legs for dressing
15 months	Builds tower of three blocks Can place small pegs in pegboard	Crawling is discarded except on stairs Plays while squatting Gets to standing position without holding on to anything	Points to object when named Points to several body parts	Fills container with blocks Scribbles with crayon without demonstration	Shows awareness/discomfort when diaper is soiled Scoops food with spoon (spills)
18 months	Builds tower of four blocks Turns pages of book, two or three at a time	Seats self in small chair Climbs stairs holding rail	Refers to self by name Puts together two-word sentences	Inserts simple shapes into a formboard	Removes socks Sometimes indicates the need to eliminate before an accident Chews semisolid foods

Continued on next page

Table 1.1 continued

Age	Fine motor	Gross motor	Speech/language	Cognitive/perceptual	Personal/social
24 months	Builds tower of seven blocks Strings small beads	Kicks a ball forward Jumps with both feet leaving floor	Produces 25–200 words Jargon has disappeared Points to pictures in book Enjoys listening to simple stories and nursery rhymes	Matches three colors Imitates strokes (circular scribble, straight vertical line) with crayon	Holds glass with two hands Has bladder control Imitates housework Drinks from straw Recognizes edible/nonedible food Helps pull down pants Finds armholes in pullover shirt
30 months	Builds tower of nine blocks Turns pages of book one at a time Shows preference for one hand	Climbs stairs with one foot to each step Stands on one foot briefly Rides tricycle	Understands taking turns	Imitates circle, horizontal stroke with crayon Names own drawings, even if unrecognizable	Uses napkin Unfastens large buttons Puts away jacket, toys Assists in pulling on socks
36 months	Builds tower of ten blocks Holds crayon with fingers like adult Cuts "fringe" with scissors	Runs on toes Runs, turning sharp corners without falling Performs broad jump about 12 inches distance	Vocabulary of about 1000 words Carries on purposeful conversation No longer repeats or echoes others	Imitates cross wich crayon Names and sorts objects by color Counts three objects correctly	Feeds self with fork, spoon, rarely spilling Zips and unzips front zipper once engaged Snaps front snaps Buttons large buttons Puts on shoes, wrong foot Turns water on/off

42 months	Can place ten pellets or raisins in small bottle within 25 seconds Shifts crayon up/down in fingers to adjust	Stands on tiptoe for ten seconds Hops on one foot		Names some letters, numbers	Puts shoes on correct foot Knows front from back of clothing Puts on mittens Can undo buckle Blows nose into tissue
4 years	Can place ten pellets or raisins in small bottle within 20 seconds Cuts 1-inch wide line within $\frac{1}{16}$ inch	Performs somersault Catches a beanbag with the hands (not against body) Performs broad jump about 24 inches distance	Can recall four digits in sequence Speech is 90% understandable	Copies square with crayon Draws one or two letters, numbers	Removes pullover garment Puts socks on correctly Washes/dries face/hands effectively Runs brush/comb through hair Places dirty clothes in hamper Sets table with help
5 years	Can place ten pellets or raisins in small bottle within 18 seconds Cuts out square within ¼ inch	Runs through obstacle course avoiding obstacles Skips with alternating swing Stands on one foot for 10 seconds		Counts ten objects correctly Prints first name Draws recognizable face with eyes, nose, mouth	Drinks from water fountain without help Serves self and carries tray in line Wipes self after toileting Dresses without supervision Ties the half knot on shoes Looks both ways to cross street Bathes/showers when reminded

Continued on next page

Table 1.1 continued

Age	Fine motor	Gross motor	Speech/language	Cognitive/perceptual	Personal/social
6 years	Can move coin from palm of hand to fingers to place in soda machine	Performs one each of sit-up and knee push-up Rides two-wheeler	Likes silly stories and riddles	Copies triangle and crude diamond Prints all letters and numbers one to nine without a model to copy Prints last name Performs simple addition and subtraction Discriminates left from right	Uses knife/fork to cut Ties bow Closes fasteners on back of clothes Cares for nose effectively Initiates phone calls to others Fastens back buttons Adjusts faucet temperature for bath
7 years			Reading and writing at school	Prints three-to-four word sentences Reversals in writing are no longer common	Styles hair Knows value of coins
8 years					Bathes/showers independently Remembers to wash ears Sweeps, mops or vacuums floors
10 years				Writes in cursive instead of printing	Ties necktie Uses stove or microwave independently Uses household cleaning agents appropriately
12 years					Uses deodorant Counts change for purchases costing more than $1.00

Sources: Baron 1996; Brigance 1978; Coley 1978; Furuno *et al.* 1984; Klein 1988; Knobloch, Stevens and Malone 1980; Santa Cruz County Office of Education 1987; Sparrow, Balla and Cicchetti 1984.

milestones later than other children, motor development is usually no more delayed than speech or cognitive development. In many children with mental retardation, the quality of movement, or coordination, is normal when compared to other children at the same developmental level. As another example, children with significant vision impairment may experience problems with coordination because they lack the visual feedback needed to orient their body in space and to guide movement.

For the purposes of this book, we will discuss the causes and classification of problems with motor development and coordination that cannot be attributed to an obvious physical problem (such as an amputation or paralyzed limb), to obvious brain damage (as in cerebral palsy or a traumatic head injury), or to global developmental delay or mental retardation. Instead, we will focus on issues that relate to children who demonstrate poor motor planning and coordination as an isolated developmental problem or as part of a specific learning disorder.

Interest in children with developmental movement problems became apparent in the literature early in the twentieth century, but was not studied scientifically until the latter half of the century. A number of authors described children who displayed difficulty performing skilled movements despite normal intelligence (Gubbay 1975; Walton, Ellis and Court 1962). Although these children demonstrated normal performance on conventional neurological examinations, they frequently exhibited a variety of qualitative neurologic differences, sometimes called neurologic soft signs, including tremors or other involuntary movements, low muscle tone, "overflow movements" such as sticking out one's tongue when cutting with scissors, or delayed development of a dominant hand. The presence of these soft signs was believed to infer a mild degree of brain dysfunction as the cause of motor difficulties. As a result, the medical community created the diagnostic label of minimal brain dysfunction to describe children with clumsiness or other specific motor execution problems. This is only one of many labels that have been used over the years to describe children with these problems. Others in popular use have included clumsy child syndrome, perceptual-motor impairment, developmental apraxia, congenital maladroitness, sensory integrative dysfunction, hyperkinetic syndrome of childhood, nonverbal learning disability, and, more recently, *dyspraxia*, which is the more commonly used term in the United Kingdom, and *developmental coordination disorder* (DCD), which is more often used in the United States. The wide variety of labels in popular use reflects the lack of agreement among professionals as to the specific causes and manifestations of mild motor impairment. It is likely that clumsiness does not represent a single disorder, but rather a heterogenous group of disorders affecting motor control. Unfortunately, this can create great confusion for parents and others who seek clear answers about the child's condition, but who hear very divergent labels, descriptions, and treatment recommendations from the various professionals they encounter. Part of the problem lies in the variability among children in terms of the severity and specific symptoms of the disorder. Some children are severely affected, and have difficulty with all forms of motor execution, while others may have very subtle difficulties, or can perform some motor tasks well and others very poorly. Another problem has to do with the assessment of motor coordination disorders. Because formal tests are designed in such a way that they can measure only a small sample of motor skills, they typically under-identify some of the more subtle qualitative aspects of motor performance. Subsequently, different professionals may apply different criteria to labeling a child as having dyspraxia or DCD (Keogh 1982).

DCD is the diagnostic label currently preferred by most professionals in the United States to describe the child with a specific motor coordination disorder, while dyspraxia is the term preferred in the United Kingdom. As described in the *Diagnostic and Statistical Manual of Mental Disorders* (DSM-IV) (American Psychiatric Association 1994, p.53) it is defined as a "marked impairment in the development of motor coordination…only if this impairment significantly interferes with academic achievement or activities of daily living…and is not due to a general medical condition." DCD can present as a specific disorder, but frequently co-exists with other diagnoses that affect learning and behavior, including mental retardation, ADHD, autism spectrum disorders (especially pervasive developmental disorder and Asperger's syndrome), and specific learning disabilities. Prevalence estimates suggest that approximately 6 percent of school-aged children may have an isolated developmental coordination disorder (Maeland 1992; Missiuna and Polatajko 1995). Furthermore, DCD often, but not always, co-exists with other learning disabilities including autism and attention deficit disorders, making coordination difficulties widely prevalent in school-aged children (Kadesjo and Gillberg 1999; Polatajko, 1999; Tarnopol and Tarnopol 1977).

The cause of DCD is not well understood. Factors that may or may not play a role include genetic predisposition, minor neurologic abnormalities, impaired information processing, or environmental impoverishment (Cermak, Gubbay and Larkin 2002). It is generally believed to be a problem involving the *cortical* (brain-directed) process of *praxis* (motor planning). Praxis involves several components including:

1. ideation, which is the ability to mentally create a motor goal and think about how to achieve that goal

2. motor planning, which is the ability to intentionally plan and sequence the motor actions needed to achieve the goal

3. motor coordination, which allows the individual to accomplish movements with precision

4. feedback, which involves recognizing whether the individual was successful in achieving the motor goal, and responding to the consequences (May-Benson 2004).

Although praxis is largely a cortical process, it is dependent on a number of subcortical (unconscious) processes involving sensory discrimination and body awareness.

In the past, many professionals have held the belief that developmental co-ordination problems do not warrant direct intervention because they may be outgrown as the children reach adolescence or adulthood. However, research has shown that this is not the case for most children (Geuze and Borger 1993; Losse *et al.* 1991). While many clumsy children appear less affected as they become older, this is most likely the result of learning to adapt to their differences as well as learning to avoid situations that may cause frustration or failure. Failure to provide help for children with coordination difficulties exposes them to the risk of failure in performing school and social activities, frustration and loss of self esteem, and ridicule and bullying by other children.

Related areas of concern

Although the main focus of this book is on addressing issues related to problems with fine and gross motor development, children with developmental coordination disorders may experience other problems related to poor motor control. Certain types of vision and speech disorders are common among these children.

Functional vision skills

Children with DCD may also experience related problems with certain aspects of vision. There are many different types of vision problems that can occur in children. Some are caused by physical abnormalities to the eye or its related structures. These may be present at birth or caused by injury or illness, and are referred to as *structural* vision problems. Blindness, cataracts, and glaucoma are examples of structural vision problems, and are not typically found in children with DCD. Other vision difficulties are caused by problems that affect the efficiency of the visual system. These are referred to as *functional* vision problems, and include such common problems as nearsightedness or farsightedness, and some less common problems impacting upon the efficient use of vision. Visual efficiency disorders occur when there are problems with eye muscle control that impact upon such skills as keeping the eyes focused on a line of print, or adjusting eye position to stay focused on a ball as it comes closer to the child. Thus, functional vision problems relate to an inability to plan and execute eye muscle movements efficiently, as opposed to a health or structural problem with the eyes, and may frequently occur in children with DCD. Functional vision disorders, especially when mild, can be hard to detect, since they may fluctuate over time and can occur in children who have perfectly normal visual acuity. Some children may complain of eyestrain, or blurred or double vision, but others fail to report problems to parents or teachers because they do not understand that those symptoms are abnormal.

Most eye doctors do not routinely screen children for these visual efficiency disorders, but focus more on eye health and visual acuity (being able to see clearly when looking at stationary visual targets at near point and at far point). Symptoms of these problems may relate to the appearance of the eyes, to behaviors observed in the child, especially during reading or other close visual work, and to complaints made by the child who experiences eyestrain as a result of inefficient vision. Table 1.2 presents symptoms that may suggest problems with functional vision (Kurtz 2006).

Table 1.2 Symptoms of visual efficiency disorders

Appearance	Eyes turn in or out
	Difficulty keeping eyes focused on a moving target (e.g. finger puppet) held about 12 inches from the eyes
	Drooping eyelids
	Crusting, swelling, redness
	Persistent tearing
	Squinting
Behaviors	Rubbing or pulling at the eyes
	Disinterest in, or avoidance of, activities requiring close visual attention
	Poor reading comprehension despite good vocabulary and spoken language skills
	Daydreaming during reading or other visual activities
	Tilting the head, or covering or closing one eye during reading
	Persistently holding reading material in an unusual position
	Skipping lines or words when reading
	Clumsiness and poor handwriting
Complaints	Frequent headaches during or following reading
	Eyes ache or burn
	Blurred or double vision
	Words disappear or "jump" during reading
	Nausea or dizziness during or following reading
	Excessive fatigue at the end of the school day

The presence of one or more of these symptoms combined with poor school achievement suggests the need for a formal vision assessment by a developmental-behavioral optometrist, who has specialized training in this area.

Even if vision is intact and works efficiently, the visual information that is transmitted to the brain must be understood and correctly interpreted by the brain. Problems with this interpretation are called problems with *visual perception*, and are common among children with autism, ADHD, and learning disabilities. Problems with visual perception will be discussed in Chapter 6.

Speech disorders

Speech requires many complex movements involving the tongue, lips, jaw, and other oral-motor structures. It is not surprising, then, that many children with coordination problems affecting other parts of their body will also have difficulty coordinating the movements necessary to make speech sounds. As with other motor skills, speech sounds develop over time, so certain substitutions are acceptable at a young age but are expected to disappear as the child matures. For example, many young children substitute the sound "f" for the sound "th," calling a bathtub "baftub," or substitute the sound "w" for "r," saying "wed" for "red." When children continue to use immature speech sounds beyond the expected age, or when their speech is hard to understand, they are said to have a speech *articulation* disorder. Fortunately, problems with articulation are usually noticed at an early age, and can be helped through speech therapy. Children with oral-motor coordination problems may also present with feeding difficulties, such as excessive drooling, choking, or unusual food preferences.

Some children with developmental coordination disorders will also have dyspraxia that affects their speech. *Praxis* is the medical term for being able to initiate and execute skilled movements. *Apraxia* means absence of this ability, and *dyspraxia* means partial absence of this ability. Poor praxis of speech is referred to by several names, but most commonly as *developmental verbal dyspraxia* or *childhood apraxia of speech* (CAS). The difference between CAS and oral-motor difficulties leading to poor articulation and/or feeding difficulties is subtle. In CAS, the child is capable of making the coordinated movements necessary for nonspeech or speech functions, but has difficulty performing these movements on demand or when consciously attending to the movements. Thus, a toddler with this problem may easily make the "ma" sound during play, but cannot respond to a request to say "mama." Often, children with CAS are aware of their difficulty, and become easily frustrated or distressed when trying to talk. There are two components of CAS, *oral apraxia* and *verbal apraxia*. In oral apraxia, the child has difficulty with intentional control over nonspeech movements, such as sticking out the tongue or smacking the lips. In verbal apraxia, the difficulty is with intentional production of speech. This can affect many areas other than just the production of sounds. Rate, rhythm, fluency, inflection, and the ability to string words together to form connected speech can all be affected. Children with oral apraxia almost always have verbal apraxia as well, but verbal apraxia may uncommonly occur without oral-motor difficulties. Problems with CAS can range from subtle to very severe, and require evaluation by a skilled speech therapist. Table 1.3 presents warning signs of problems with speech or oral-motor skills.

Table 1.3 Signs of possible oral-motor/speech problems

Difficulty nursing or bottle-drinking during infancy

Open mouth posture, even without a stuffy nose

Excessive drooling

Tongue protrusion

Poor speech intelligibility

Difficulty imitating funny faces or mouth games

Limited ability to show emotion in facial expression

Strong food preferences, picky eater, slow to finish a meal

Overstuffing food in the mouth

Swallowing without chewing

Grinding teeth

References

American Psychiatric Association (1994) *Diagnostic and Statistical Manual (4th Edition)*. Washington, DC: APA.

Baron, M.A. (1996) "Language and Speech." In L.A. Kurtz, P.W. Dowrick, S.E. Levy and M.L. Batshow (eds) *Handbook of Developmental Disabilities: Resources for Interdisciplinary Care* (pp.44–45). Gaithersburg, MD: Aspen.

Brigance, A.H. (1978) *Inventory of Early Development*. North Billerica, MA: Curriculum Associates, Inc.

Cermak, S.A., Gubbay, S.S. and Larkin, D. (2002) "What is Developmental Coordination Disorder?" In S.A. Cermak and D. Larkin (eds) *Developmental Coordination Disorder* (pp.2–22). Albany, NY: Delmar.

Coley, I.L. (1978) *Pediatric Assessment of Self-Care Activities*. St. Louis, MO: C.V. Mosby Co.

Furuno, S., O'Reilly, K.A., Hosaka, C.M. *et al.* (1984) *Hawaii Early Learning Profile (HELP)*. Palo Alto, CA: VORT Corporation.

Geuze, R. and Borger, H. (1993) "Children who are clumsy: Five years later." *Adaptive Physical Activity Quarterly 10*, 10–21.

Gubbay, S.S. (1975) *The Clumsy Child*. London: W.B. Saunders.

Kadesjo, B. and Gillberg, C. (1999) "Developmental coordination disorder in Swedish seven-year-old children." *Journal of the American Academy of Child and Adolescent Psychiatry 38*, 7, 820–828.

Keogh, J.F. (1982) "The Study of Movement Learning Disabilities." In J.P. Das, R.F. Mulcahy and A.E. Wall (eds) *Theory and Research in Learning Disabilities* (pp.237–251). New York, NY: Plenum Press.

Klein, M.D. (1988) *Pre-Dressing Skills*. Tucson, AZ: Therapy Skill Builders.

Knobloch, H., Stevens, F. and Malone, A.F. (1980) *Manual of Developmental Diagnosis, Revised Edition*. New York, NY: Harper and Row.

Kurtz, L.A. (2006) *Visual Perception Problems in Children with AD/HD, Autism, and Other Learning Disabilities: A Guide for Parents and Professionals*. London, UK: Jessica Kingsley Publishers.

Losse, A., Henderson, S.A., Elliman, D., Hall, D. *et al.* (1991) "Clumsiness in children: Do they outgrow it? A 10-year follow-up study." *Developmental Medicine and Child Neurology 33*, 55–68.

Maeland, A.F. (1992) "Identification of children with motor coordination problems." *Adapted Physical Education Quarterly 9*, 330–342.

May-Benson, T.A. (2004) "Praxis is more than just motor planning." *American Journal of Occupational Therapy 9*, 18, CE 1–8.

Missiuna, C. and Polatajko, H. (1995) "Developmental dyspraxia by any other name: Are they all just clumsy children?" *American Journal of Occupational Therapy 49*, 7, 619–627.

Piaget, J. and Inhelder, B. (1969) *The Psychology of the Child*. New York, NY: Basic Books.

Polatajko, H.J. (1999) "Developmental coordination disorder (DCD): Alias the Clumsy Child Syndrome." In K. Whitmore, H. Hart and G. Willems (eds) *A Neurodevelopmental Approach to Specific Learning Disabilities: Clinics in Developmental Medicine, no. 45* (pp.119–133). London: MacKeith Press.

Santa Cruz County Office of Education (1987) *HELP for Special Preschoolers: Assessment Checklist*. Palo Alto, CA: VORT Corporation.

Sparrow, S.S., Balla, D.A. and Cicchetti, D.V. (1984) *Vineland Adaptive Behavior Scales: Survey Form Manual, Interview Edition*. Circle Pines, MN: American Guidance Service.

Tarnopol, L. and Tarnopol, M. (1977) *Brain Function and Reading Disabilities*. Baltimore, MD: University Park Press.

Walton, J.N., Ellis, E. and Court, S. (1962) "Clumsy children: Developmental apraxia and agnosia." *Brain 85*, 603–612.

Chapter 2

FINDING PROFESSIONAL HELP

Parents are notoriously excellent observers of their own child's strengths and weaknesses, even when they lack formal training about what should be expected of a "normally" developing child. Because parents see their child playing and interacting on a daily basis with other children, they are usually the first to observe that their child is more awkward than his or her peers. For this reason, unless the child has a specific medical condition that places him or her at risk for developmental delay, it is often the parent, and not a teacher or pediatrician, who first expresses concern about the child's development and ability to function. Sometimes, especially when coordination difficulties are very mild, it is not until the child enters school that these difficulties are recognized as interfering enough with the child's function to warrant some type of help. This is not surprising considering that an estimated 30 to 60 percent of a child's day in elementary school is devoted to activities which require some type of fine motor performance involving using a pencil or scissors or working with manipulatives (McHale and Cermak 1992). Sometimes, when a child has been diagnosed with a potentially serious disability such as autism or ADHD, parents are focused on the more pressing issues raised by the diagnosis, and place motor coordination issues lower on their list of priorities. But at what point should parents consider clumsiness to be enough of a problem to warrant a formal evaluation? And how can they go about finding the most appropriate methods for evaluation? When is it necessary to consult a pediatric neurologist or other medical specialist? How do they know that the professionals they select have sufficient knowledge of developmental disabilities and the various treatment options to be nonbiased and genuinely helpful?

Parents who are concerned about any aspect of their child's development, including motor development, should first discuss these concerns with the child's pediatrician. It is important to be explicit in describing the problem leading to the referral, and to provide detailed examples of how motor difficulties are affecting the child's ability to succeed in performing daily tasks, or to cope emotionally with age-appropriate challenges. Some parents find it helpful to keep a log which details problems observed during the child's play and self care to present to the doctor. The level of frustration experienced by the child is often a very revealing clue as to the significance of the motor difficulty. For example, the three-year-old who has absolutely no interest in learning to ride a tricycle may present less of a problem than the three-year-old who is highly motivated to learn, but fails and becomes frustrated even given frequent opportunities to practice. The pediatrician will perform a screening assessment of the child's overall developmental maturity. Based upon these preliminary findings, he or she will determine the need for any further evaluation of medical concerns that could contribute to motor difficulties, and may request consultation from one or more medical specialists such as a neurologist, orthopedist, or geneticist. He or she may also recommend that a more comprehensive developmental evaluation be conducted. Because some pediatricians believe that children will "outgrow" motor coordination difficulties, they may advise parents to withhold formal testing or intervention until the child is older or is showing very significant functional limitations. This "wait and see" approach may not be in the best interest of the child and the family who must cope with his or her frustrations. Parents should not hesitate to request a second opinion if the pediatrician agrees that the child has delays but does not suggest referral for further testing, or is not able to adequately respond to the parents' questions and concerns.

In the United States, federal legislation (Education of the Handicapped Amendments of 1986, or Public Law 99-457, Part H) provides for free early intervention services for children up to age three who meet eligibility requirements, which vary from state to state. Children with developmental motor concerns may or may not be eligible for services, such as free therapy, through this system. Early intervention programs typically provide multidisciplinary developmental assessment at the time the child enrolls in the program. Often, referrals for evaluation are initiated by pediatricians or preschool educators, but parents should be aware that they can request an evaluation on their own. Keep in mind, however, that the purpose of this evaluation is to determine eligibility for services, not to make a medical diagnosis, nor to predict the child's future developmental potential. If the child's difficulties appear to be significant, it may be prudent to seek comprehensive developmental evaluation through a medical setting such as a pediatric hospital prior to, or concurrent with, enrollment in early intervention. Such assessment may help to answer questions about the child's prognosis and how to plan for the future.

In the United States, federal legislation (the Individuals with Disabilities Education Act (IDEA), or Public Law 101-76 of 1990 and its reauthorizations in 1991, 1997 and 2004) provides for free special education and support services for children between the ages of three and 21. In most states, the local school district is responsible for providing these services. Children with developmental motor concerns may be eligible for services, including therapy, if they meet their state's eligibility requirements for classification as a special education student. In addition, some children with disabilities who do not require special education (for example, a child with ADHD who is bright and is meeting academic expectations in school) may be eligible for services under other entitlements, such as the Americans with Disabilities Act (ADA) of 1990, or Section 504 of the Rehabilitation Act of 1973. Up until fairly recently, the child needed to demonstrate a significant degree of delay or adverse effect from his or her disability in order to qualify for services at school. Now, schools recognize that it is sometimes beneficial to offer a student extra help in the form of preventative therapy or support within the mainstream classroom even before identifying the student as needing special education. However, parents are cautioned that services provided within the school setting tend to be limited in their scope. Only those therapy services needed to support the student's educational needs are provided for under the legislation. Schools are not required to provide therapy services that might support the child's participation at home or in the community.

Similar provisions are provided to children in the United Kingdom. A government code of practice, the Special Educational Needs and Disability Act 2001, offers guidance to local education authorities and state schools on how to identify, assess, and monitor students with special learning needs. As in the United States, an effort is made to teach in schools in the mainstream setting to the greatest extent possible. Children with special learning needs may have an individual action plan developed by their local school. For those students who need more help than the local school can provide, the local authority draws up a statement of special educational needs which can offer extra help, usually on-site at the school.

Typically, frequency and intensity of school-based therapy, as well as the amount of direct parent instruction, are more limited than may be available through hospitals or other providers of therapy such as private clinics. Some parents choose to augment the services their child receives through school by seeing a private therapist who can devote more time and attention to parent training and support.

In whatever setting an evaluation occurs, a comprehensive developmental assessment uses multiple methods of data collection, typically including a thorough interview of parents and other significant caregivers, evaluation of physical and neurological function, a structured observation of the child at play, and the use of one or more standardized developmental assessment tools. This comprehensive approach is important because no single method of assessment is completely free of error or bias. When more than one measure is used to make a diagnosis, the likelihood of error is reduced. Ideally, the evaluation of children with significant motor or other developmental concerns will be conducted by a team of developmental specialists under the direction of a doctor who specializes in the care of children with problems affecting development, such as a pediatric neurologist or a developmental pediatrician. A developmental pediatrician is a board-certified pediatrician who has completed three years of pediatrics residency followed by three years of developmental pediatrics fellowship. This training provides for advanced skills in the evaluation and management of children with developmental or behavioral disabilities. The developmental pediatrician will assume responsibility for integrating evaluation information from a variety of sources so that an accurate diagnosis can be made. This person will also help the team to develop a coordinated plan for intervention that addresses the parent's concerns and priorities. Developmental pediatricians often work in major pediatric teaching hospitals. The Association of University Centers on Disability (AUCD), included in Appendix III, can provide suggestions for referral sources throughout the United States.

It is usually helpful to involve professionals from several professions in the comprehensive developmental evaluation, because the team members will bring different perspectives to the evaluation process, resulting in a more comprehensive interpretation of the findings. Exactly which professionals need to be involved depends on the specific concerns raised about the child. Table 2.1 summarizes the roles and functions of various professionals and medical subspecialists who may participate in a comprehensive developmental evaluation.

For children with mild developmental motor concerns, evaluation by a therapist skilled in the assessment of motor development and quality of movement is essential. Occupational therapists are particularly well qualified in this area, although some physical therapists also specialize in working with children with mild motor difficulties. The primary focus of occupational therapy (OT) is to address problems with fine motor and perceptual development that interfere with self care, play, and school performance, which are the primary "occupations" of childhood. Physical therapy (PT) addresses problems with gross motor development and the ability to be mobile within the environment. Appendix I provides a list of tests and assessments that are commonly used for children with motor coordination and related problems.

Table 2.1 Professionals involved in evaluation of children with developmental motor concerns

Professional	Typical services provided	Qualifications	When referral is indicated
Audiologist	Perform hearing tests Obtain hearing aids or other devices	Master's degree Clinical fellowship year (CFY) National certification exam	Delayed speech or language Parent concerns about hearing Recurrent ear infections
Developmental or behavioral optometrist	Assess eye health, acuity, and functional vision skills Provide interventions that may include vision therapy to address problems with visual efficiency	Completion of a four-year graduate program leading to a Doctor of Optometry (OD) Completion of postgraduate examination by one of two organizations: 1. American Academy of Optometry or 2. College of Optometrists in Vision Development	Physical signs of eyestrain Poor reading comprehension despite good vocabulary and speech Blurred or double vision Frequently losing place during reading Avoidance of visual activities
Developmental pediatrician	Diagnosis and medical management of developmental delay	Board certified pediatrician Three-year fellowship in developmental pediatrics	Suspected developmental disorder Conflict of opinion regarding diagnosis or management of developmental concerns
Geneticist	Testing to determine presence of inherited diseases	Medical degree Fellowship and board certification in genetics	Congenital malformations or stigmata Family history of mental retardation, genetic disease, chromosome abnormality, known or suspected syndrome

Provider	Role	Requirements	Indications
Neurologist (pediatric)	Evaluation and management of nervous system disorders	Medical degree Residency in pediatric neurology Board certification	Loss or plateau of developmental skill Known or suspected seizures Unknown etiology of developmental disability
Occupational therapist	Evaluation and management of problems performing daily living skills	Occupational therapist: BS or MS in occupational therapy Board certification Licensure (varies by state) Advanced pediatric certification available for pediatrics, sensory integration, or neurodevelopmental therapy *OT assistant (OTA):* AS in occupational therapy Board certification Licensure (varies by state) Must be supervised by occupational therapist	Limited ability to succeed in daily activities Limited mobility, especially fine motor Poorer nonverbal than verbal development Frustration leading to task avoidance, poor attention, or problems with social interactions
Physical therapist	Evaluation and management of problems with mobility	Physical therapist: BS or MS in physical therapy Board certification Licensure (varies by state) Advanced pediatric certification available for pediatrics, sensory integration, or neurodevelopmental therapy	Delayed gross motor development or abnormal movement quality

Continued on next page

Table 2.1 continued

Professional	Typical services provided	Qualifications	When referral is indicated
		PT assistant (PTA): AS in physical therapy Board certification Licensure (varies by state) Must be supervised by physical therapist	
Psychiatrist	Evaluation and management of emotional disorders	Medical degree Residency (pediatrics, internal medicine, and/or psychiatry) Board certification	Suspected impairment in emotions or thought processes Serious behavioral or adjustment problems
Psychologist	Evaluation of cognitive capabilities and potential Measurement of academic achievement and educational needs Evaluation and management of problematic behavior	*Psychologist:* Doctoral degree in psychology Internship and fellowship (varies by state) State licensure *School psychologist:* Master's degree in psychology Supervised field experience State licensure National certification exam (NCSP)	Undiagnosed developmental delay Decline/regression in skill development School performance poorer than expected Inappropriate or atypical behavior

Professional	Role	Training/Requirements	Indications
Social worker	Provide support to child and family around social and emotional adjustment Assist family to identify and access community services or entitlements	Master's degree in social work Licensure (some states) Advanced certification available (ACSW)	Suspected child abuse or neglect Acute distress in child or family Chronic stress related to caregiving responsibilities Poor parental adjustment to diagnosis Assistance needed for referral, access, or funding for services
Special educator	Design and implementation of specialized programs of educational instruction	Minimum requirements: Bachelor's degree in education One semester supervised student teaching Certifications (e.g. early childhood, reading specialist): Varies by state	Child meets eligibility requirements as defined by state for early intervention or special education
Speech language pathologist	Evaluation and management of problems with communication	Master's degree in speech/language pathology Clinical fellowship year (CFY) National certification exam Licensure (some states)	Delay or impairment in communication skills Problems with oral-motor coordination affecting speech

When choosing tests, therapists attempt to identify well-designed tools that will help them to make appropriate clinical decisions. Because no test is perfect, scores should not be used to make clinical decisions unless they are consistent with the therapist's clinical observations and overall impression of the child. Tests may be described as either criterion-referenced or standardized. Criterion-referenced tests measure the child's performance according to an established standard, and are used more for screening or descriptive purposes than as a true measure of ability. Standardized tests are tests that have been developed so that procedures, materials, and scoring techniques are used in exactly the same way each time the test is given. This ensures that there is uniformity across test subjects. The child's score is then compared to those obtained by a group of test subjects who have comparable qualities (age, grade level, socioeconomic status, etc.). By looking at the scores obtained on standardized tests, the therapist can see how the child is performing relative to other children. Table 2.2 provides an overview of different types of test scores that may be included in an evaluation report so that you can understand what the numbers mean.

When motor difficulties are mild, parents and professionals alike may struggle with deciding the appropriateness of therapy. Unfortunately, therapy is not an exact science, and there are no strict guidelines for when and when not to provide therapy. Some children outgrow the problem, at least to a certain degree, so some professionals advocate delaying therapy for very young children until their developmental course is clearer. An alternative point of view, however, is that younger children may benefit most from intervention, since they are developing so rapidly, and since early childhood education programs place such high emphasis on activities that require a coordinated motor response. Early intervention can also address problems with self confidence and self esteem which commonly occur in children with poor motor skills, and which can lead to avoidance behaviors that further impact upon motor skills development. If therapy is recommended, parents should evaluate all options before enrolling in a program. Possible sources of information for locating skilled therapists in the area may be obtained through the rehabilitation department of a local pediatric hospital, through local universities that train therapists, or by contacting the professional organizations listed in Appendix III included at the end of this book. Parents should be encouraged to interview or visit several therapists, evaluating such qualities as the therapists' training and experience with children who have similar conditions, the convenience and affordability of the program, and the rapport established between therapist, parent, and child. Parents should contribute to setting the goals for therapy, and should have a clear understanding of when and how those goals should be achieved. Parents should be reminded that effective therapy is a collaborative

Table 2.2 Descriptions of test scores

Description	Score
Raw score	The number of test items the subject completed successfully. In a criterion-referenced test, the raw score may be reported or reported as the percentage of items passed. For standardized tests, the raw score has little meaning until it has been converted using a variety of statistical procedures.
Percentile	The percentage of scores that were below the child's score. If the child scored at the 75th percentile, he or she scored as well as, or better than, 75% of children in the normative group. A drawback in using percentiles is that there is inequality between percentile units, with a larger difference at the ends of the scale than in the middle. Therefore, there is a greater difference in performance between the 90th and 95th percentile than there is between the 50th and 55th percentile.
Standard deviation	A numerical index that indicates how widely spread the scores were for the normative group. In a normally distributed bell curve, 68.3% of subjects will score within one standard deviation of the mean (-1.0 SD to $+1.0$ SD), and 95.4% will score within two standard deviations of the mean (-2.0 to $+2.0$).
Standard scores	There are a number of different formulas for using the standard deviation to convert to different types of standard scores. For example, a standard score may be based upon a mean of 100 and a standard deviation of 15, meaning that scores ranging from 85 to 100 are considered average. A *T-Score* is a type of standard score adjusted to have a mean of 50 and a standard deviation of 10, so scores ranging from 40 to 60 would be considered average. A *stanine* is a standard score with a range of 1–9, where 5 is the mean and the standard deviation is 2. Thus, stanines of 3–7 are considered average.
Age equivalent scores	The average age of children in the normative group who achieved the same raw score as the child. Although age-equivalent scores seem easy to understand, they are easily over-interpreted. A major limitation is that most skills measured by tests do not increase incrementally by the same amount each year. For example, most children show more gains in gross motor skills between the ages of one and two than between the ages of 15 and 16.

undertaking between parent and therapist, requiring significant time and effort toward planning, participation, and evaluation of outcome. They should remember that "more" therapy is not always better, since time spent in therapy is time taken away from other activities that could also be important to the child. Obviously, parents will benefit from having objective measures to indicate that therapy is effective in addressing their concerns. Table 2.3 suggests the qualities you should expect of a good therapy program.

Table 2.3 Qualities of a good therapy program

The therapist:

- Treats you and your child with respect
- Sets a positive tone during therapy sessions
- Has the appropriate training and experience
- Communicates regularly and in a way you can understand
- Includes you in all decisions regarding your child
- Willingly communicates with other professionals involved with your child
- Knows what he or she can/cannot accomplish, helping you find other help if necessary
- Is effective in helping your child to learn

The therapy program:

- Is based on principles that have been explained to you
- Includes specific goals that you understand and have agreed upon
- Includes a projected time frame for achievement of goals
- Provides regular, written reports of progress and current recommendations
- Includes home/school recommendations that are realistic to manage

The therapy environment:

- Is clean and safe
- Includes a wide variety of toys and materials available for therapy

The child:

- Relates well with the therapist, and finds most activities enjoyable
- Makes observable changes in performance or behavior

If you are not satisfied with the results, discuss your concerns openly with the therapist. If you are not able to negotiate change to your satisfaction, seek help elsewhere. Many parents are afraid to complain to a therapist or to change therapists, fearing that they will appear to be disloyal. Remember that the only loyalty you have is to your child, and it is up to you to see that he or she gets the proper help!

Many parents are uncomfortable with deciding what to tell the child who needs an evaluation or therapy services. It is important to be honest with the child, and to express the concerns leading to the evaluation in simple terms that are meaningful to the child. Remember that the things that are important to a child are usually different from the things that are important to adults. For the preschooler, an explanation like "We're going to a doctor who wants to play some special games with you. She wants to show you some puzzles, and see how you can draw pictures. I think it will be fun for you," may suffice. For an older child who is more self aware of his or her problems, an explanation like "We're going to a special teacher to see if she has some ideas about how to help you learn handwriting more easily" might be better. Most evaluators are skilled with putting the child at ease, and it is uncommon for the child to find testing an unpleasant experience. In fact, most children seem to enjoy the personal attention received during the evaluation process.

References

Americans with Disabilities Act (ADA) of 1990, PL 101-336, 42 U.S.C. §§ 12101 *et seq.*

Education of the Handicapped Amendments of 1986, PL 99-457, 20 U.S.C. §§ 1400.

Individuals with Disabilities Education Act (IDEA) of 1990, PL 101-476, 20 U.S.C. §§ 1400 *et seq.*

Individuals with Disabilities Education Act Amendments of 1991, PL 102-119, 20 U.S.C. §§ 1400 *et seq.*

Individuals with Disabilities Education Act Amendments of 1997, PL 105-17, 20 U.S.C. §§ 1400 *et seq.*

Individuals with Disabilities Education Improvement Act (IDEIA) of 2004, PL 108-446, 20, U.S.C. §§ 1400 *et seq.*

McHale, K. and Cermak, S.A. (1992) "Fine motor activities in elementary school: Preliminary findings and provisional implications for children with fine motor problems." *American Journal of Occupational Therapy 46*, 10, 898–903.

Rehabilitation Act of 1973, PL 93-112, 29, U.S.C. §§ 701 *et seq.*

Chapter 3

GENERAL PRINCIPLES
FOR INTERVENTION

Just as there is more than one way to teach a child to learn to read, there are many different ways to help children with problems affecting motor skills to develop improved coordination. A number of approaches are commonly used, some that are derived from basic principles of occupational or physical therapy, and others that are similar to those used by teachers or special educators to help children develop age-appropriate skills and behaviors. This section will review some of the principles behind common approaches used by therapists and other specialists for intervention.

Developmental readiness for learning motor skills

Developmental theory is based on the understanding that human development proceeds in an orderly, sequential manner, and at a rate that is reasonably predictable for the average child. Typical developmental motor milestones were discussed in Chapter 1. As a review, most children sit at about six months of age, crawl at about nine months, take their first steps at about 12 months, and begin to climb stairs at about 18 months. Therapists and other specialists who study child development know that these familiar developmental milestones are made up of even smaller steps and stages, so that virtually all behaviors can be placed in a sort of timeline, allowing us to predict when each behavior might emerge.

Furthermore, we know that there are several basic concepts governing the direction of motor development within the human body. The first of these is *cephalocaudal progression*, meaning that purposeful control of movement generally develops starting at the head (cephalo) and moving toward the tail (caudal) end of the body. Babies learn to lift and control their heads long before they can control the hips well enough to stand or walk. At the same time, there is *proximal-distal devel-*

opment, meaning that motor control develops from the midline of the body outwards toward the fingers. In the arms, control develops first at the shoulders (proximal), and gradually outwards toward the hands and fingers (distal). In the hand, control develops in an *ulnar-radial direction*, meaning that the baby first learns to grasp using the pinky side of the hand (ulnar), with controlled grasp moving gradually toward the thumb side of the hand (radial). This is an especially important concept for understanding the development of fine motor control, since the ulnar side of the hand is most important for strength and stabilization of grasp, and the radial side is most important for dexterity of hand movements. Many parents of children with fine motor delays are perplexed by the observation that their clumsy child seems to have normal or even better than average strength. In fact, it is fairly typical for strength to develop before control. Also, during moments of frustration, some children will try to use strength to substitute for motor control. Imagine, if you will, a child who throws a ball with all his might when he cannot aim with precision, or the child who scribbles aggressively using the whole hand to grasp a crayon when he cannot form the letters to write his name.

Finally, movement develops from mass patterns to more refined specific patterns. You have probably observed that a baby's first grasp of a toy uses the whole hand and is very tenuous. As development proceeds, he or she learns to use a variety of hand positions and finger patterns to grasp objects more purposefully. Thus a key and a pair of tweezers, both very small objects, are grasped slightly differently according to how they will be used. Furthermore, grasp will need to undergo subtle changes as an object is used to accomplish different purposes within different environments. When manipulating a key, for example, most of us position our fingers differently for a lock high on a door than for a trapdoor on the floor, and for a heavy door lock requiring a good deal of pressure than for the delicate lock on a jewelry box.

Current theory recognizes that development represents the combined influence of biological factors and environmental experiences. Therefore, a variety of influences—such as disease, injury, an inadequately supportive environment, or psychologically traumatic experiences—might interrupt the normal process of development. We also know that psychological factors have a strong influence on motor development. Children who are curious about exploring their environment, who seek out and enjoy physical challenges, and who possess a strong enough ego to keep on trying when they fail, will develop motor skills more easily than those children who lack these attributes.

Therapists using a developmental frame of reference to guide therapy evaluate the child's current level of development in all areas, and anticipate what should be the next step or steps in the typical developmental sequence. Next, the therapist attempts to identify any biological or environmental factors that might be corrected or modified to enhance the child's potential for success in the next small stage of development. Activities are planned in order to pose a small developmental challenge, and to be motivating and fun for the child. Specific goals for therapy are determined based on the priorities of the parents or child, the social implications of the child's environment, and the therapist's estimate of what is achievable. For example, let's say that the parents of a five-year-old girl with fine motor delays are anxious to have her hold a pencil properly so that she can write her name in school. The therapist may determine that the child is developmentally at a stage where she can crudely grasp a writing tool, but not control it well enough to make the appropriate strokes to form letters. The school's priority may be for the child to participate with her classmates during desk work so that she can benefit from the exposure to language arts and be included in joining with her peers in an activity that has other social implications for learning. In this situation, the therapist might recommend for the child to participate in desk activities at school in a modified form. For example, if the child recognizes but cannot draw letters, she might be asked to use a large, easy-to-grasp crayon to circle or place a mark on the letters in her name, instead of drawing them independently. Meanwhile, the therapist might work separately on helping the child to refine her grasp and to learn how to control strokes according to the typical developmental sequence. (Most children learn to copy vertical strokes first, then horizontal, then circles, then combinations of strokes as in a cross.) Once this is mastered, the child should more easily use those strokes to form letters.

Children whose developmental differences include problems with cognition may also benefit from a developmental intervention technique called chaining. In chaining, the therapist selects a task to be learned, then breaks it down according to each small step required to complete the task. For example, the steps involved in tying a shoelace include holding one lace in each hand, crossing lace A over lace B, then going under lace B to form a half-knot, then pulling both laces taut, then making a loop with lace A and pinching it tight at its base, then going around the loop with lace B to form a ring, then poking lace B through the ring to form a second loop, then pulling both loops simultaneously to bring the bow taut. No wonder children have trouble learning this very complicated task!

Using a forward chaining approach, the therapist helps the child to learn the first step of the sequence by himself or herself, then completes the remaining steps for the child, providing a role model for the child to observe. Once the child has mastered the first step, he or she is expected to complete the first two steps, and so forth until the task is mastered. If the child has significant cognitive or memory problems, the therapist might instead choose a reverse chaining or backwards chaining approach. Here, the child and therapist do the task together with the child assisting as much as he or she is able, but the child is then expected to complete the last step independently, then the last two steps, and so on. This technique seems to be preferable for some children with poor memory skills. For these children, it is easiest for them to remember the last step of the sequence because it is the most recent event in their memory.

It is important to understand that skills taught in this manner may or may not generalize to other situations. For example, the fact that the child learns to tie her shoes using a chaining technique does not necessarily mean she will be able to generalize that knowledge to tying other bows (for example, a sash on the back of a dress, or a ribbon on a birthday present). Each task presents its own unique context that determines the necessary steps to complete a sequence. For example, tying a sash behind the back requires doing so without vision, and with the wrists and forearms positioned differently than in shoe-tying. Tying a bow on a package requires manipulating a ribbon that probably has a very different texture and width than a shoestring, requiring subtle differences in how the fingers are used.

Sensory aspects of motor learning

One of the most important factors in how children develop motor control is the way in which they use their various senses to guide their learning. Most people are familiar with the senses of sight, hearing, touch, smell and taste, and have at least a general appreciation for how these senses might help children to learn. Obviously, children need to see and recognize the shapes of letters if they are to read, and must hear and understand words if they are to communicate. To understand the full impact of the senses on learning, it is important to understand the difference between the terms sensory reception and sensory perception. Sensory reception refers to the process that occurs when an organ of sensation (for example, the eyes or the ears) is stimulated by an event (such as a visual image or a sound). Examples of children with sensory receptive disorders might include a child with blindness or deafness. When the receptor organ is intact, it relays sensory information through the nervous system to the brain, where the information can then be attended to, organized, and used to make a plan of action. Perception refers to this ability of the brain to make sense of the information that has been transmitted via the organ of reception.

Although reception and perception problems can occur together, we usually think of children with perceptual difficulties resulting from autism, ADHD, or other learning disabilities as having normal sensory organs and normal transmission of sensory information to the brain. For reasons not well understood, the brain of a child with perceptual problems has difficulty making sense of the infor-mation that is transmitted.

Perceptual difficulties can exist with any of the senses. For example, a child with visual perceptual difficulties may have trouble recognizing shapes or letters, or may have trouble attending to details in a complicated or "busy" picture. A child with auditory perceptual difficulties may be unusually distracted by extraneous sounds, or may have trouble learning the correct sounds for speech, and the letter/sound associations needed to learn to read. Perception through sight (visual perception) and through touch (tactile perception) are known to play especially important roles in the development of motor skills. But there are other important senses that are felt on a more subconscious level, and are therefore not as well understood.

The *vestibular* sense is designed to provide the brain with information about gravity and motion, and plays a role in developing balance as well as helping to coordinate movements of the eyes, head and body. The vestibular system is complex anatomically (see Figure 3.1).

Figure 3.1 Location of the vestibular system

Located within the inner ear, it comprises two structures. The *otoliths* (saccule and utricle) contain tiny crystals attached to hair-like nerves that move in response to gravity, vibration, or subtle changes in head position, thus sending impulses to the brain. The three sets of *semicircular canals* are filled with fluid as well as hair-like cells, and are each oriented in a different direction. Rapid motion, such as that produced by jumping, rolling down a hill, or riding down a hill on a sled, causes the fluid to surge through one or more of the canals, disrupting the position of the hair-nerves and sending information about the nature of the motion to the brain.

The vestibular sense is one of the earliest sensory systems to develop, maturing by about the fifth month of gestation. Sensation from the vestibular system influences many other aspects of a child's behavior and learning, therefore contributing to development in many ways. For example, it can help to promote an alert state needed for learning, contribute to the coordination of eye movements, contribute to the way the two sides of the body coordinate their movements, and influence muscle tone throughout the body.

The *proprioceptive* system is perhaps equally important to the development of motor skills. It is a complex anatomical system consisting of various receptors located in the joints, muscles, and tendons that provide the child with a subconscious awareness of body position and body movements. For example, if you were to suddenly close your eyes, you could still "feel" whether your arms are crossed in front of your chest, hanging down by your side, or resting in your lap. Proprioceptive sensations are constantly bombarding the brain, providing the information needed to allow subtle adjustments to body positions as we move. For example, imagine that you are getting ready for your morning shower, and step into the tub leading with your right foot. It is your vision that tells the brain whether your right foot is aimed in the right direction, and whether it will land inside the shower stall. However, to maintain balance during the movement, your body also needs to shift weight to the left leg and tilt the trunk slightly to the left. Without any conscious effort on your part, proprioceptive input from the leg and trunk tell the brain how much adjustment is not too much or too little, but just right.

Sensory processes also play an important role in shaping a child's behavior and emotional tone. As the child is constantly bombarded with information from the environment and from within, he or she must learn how to attend to what is appropriate, and how to tune out what is not helpful information for the present situation. This process of selectively attending to sensory information is called sensory modulation.

Consider the following example. Most of us have had the experience of arriving at a party where there are many strangers bustling about, blaring music from an entertainer, and friends who notice our arrival and try to engage us in conversation over a background of chaos. Our initial response may be to feel a little bit overwhelmed; we may have trouble paying attention to the people who speak to us, or we may startle at loud blasts from the band or from people bumping into us as they navigate the room. Some people are so sensitive to this type of sensory experience that they may actually feel physical discomfort or great emotional distress. However, after a short while, most of us find ourselves accommodating to the situation. The noise level appears less offensive when we tune out distractions as needed to converse with our friends. In short, we relax and start to have a good time. We have modulated the sensory environment so that we can more effectively use the sensory experiences to our advantage.

Everyone's ability to modulate sensory information varies during different times of the day or under different circumstances. When we have just woken up in the morning, or are tired or sick, we may be less easily aroused by sensation than at other times. When we are excited or stressed, we may react more strongly to sensation. To use the previous example, if we attend the party after a long day at work, when we are worried about the children we left with babysitters, and with a strong desire to put on a good appearance to the other guests, our arousal level may be heightened and we may be overly sensitive to the environment. Alternatively, if we attend the party as an afterthought "just to have a good time" and are comfortable interacting with the other guests, we are likely to be more relaxed and to tune out more of the distractions with ease.

Many children with perceptual difficulties have problems with sensory modulation. They may demonstrate a low arousal level (hyporesponsive), a high arousal level (hyperresponsive), or their arousal level may fluctuate from high to low. Some children who are hyporesponsive appear to be very passive, since it takes a lot of stimulation to "get them going." They may appear to be unusually tired, lazy, or reluctant to join in activities. However, other children with hyposensitivity appear overly active. Because they have some awareness that they need stronger than average sensory input to maintain their attention, they seek out opportunities to get the sensation their nervous system craves, through touching, moving, manipulating. Many children who are hyperresponsive tend to be very active and to lack impulse control. Their nervous system is unable to screen out extraneous stimuli, or may interpret stimuli as threatening when they are not. They commonly demonstrate such behavioral characteristics as short tempers, impulsive behavior, and difficulty forming relationships with peers as they avoid potentially uncomfortable experiences. However, other children with hypersensitivity appear overly passive. With the awareness that they can become easily overwhelmed, they have taught themselves to avoid any situation that might bombard their system with sensory input and cause distress.

As adults, most of us have learned a variety of strategies for maintaining an appropriate arousal level. We do this unconsciously by modifying our sensory environment so that we create exactly the milieu we need to remain calm and attentive. For example, if you find yourself falling asleep during a long car trip, you may turn up the radio, chew on a piece of gum, and open the window to get a blast of fresh air. Loud noises, resistive physical movement, and cold temperatures are all sensory inputs that have an arousing effect for most people. Alternatively, if we have just had a fight with a good friend, and need to calm down so we can "talk things out," we may sit in a favorite rocking chair with a warm cup of tea, listening to some relaxing music while we gather our thoughts. Slow, rhythmic movement, warm temperatures, and quiet music tend to inhibit our arousal level and help to create a relaxed state. Although each child has his or her own unique way of responding to sensation, Table 3.1 presents some examples of sensory inputs that commonly produce either a calming or an arousing effect for most children.

By experimenting with different sensory inputs, you can gradually learn the type of environment that helps your child to achieve an appropriate level of arousal so he or she can optimally learn. Therapists call this creating a "sensory diet" that helps the child to react appropriately to his or her own nervous system.

Table 3.1 Typical sensory responses

Sensation	Arousing input	Calming input
Touch	Gentle, light touch	Firm touch or holding
	Tickling	Hugging
	Soft textures	Firm stroking, in direction of hair growth
	Unexpected touch	
Movement	Fast movement	Slow movement
	Bouncing	Rocking
	Jumping	Swaying
	Spinning	Moving against resistance (pushing, pulling, carrying heavy objects)
	Rolling	
Gravity	Head upright when sitting or standing	Head supported, leaning either forward or back
Sound	Loud or exciting music	Soft or gentle music
	Loud or sudden noises	Quiet, rhythmic sounds
	Unexpected changes in pitch or tone	
Vision	"Busy" or complicated decor	Few visual distractions
	Bright lights or colors	Indirect, low-intensity light
	Objects in motion	
Taste	Salty, spicy, sour foods	Sweet or bland foods
	Crunchy textures	Chewy textures
		Sucking through a straw
Temperature	Very cold or very hot	Warm, moderate temperature
Smell	Strong or noxious odors	Familiar odors
	Unfamiliar odors	

For example, the child with ADHD who is easily overwhelmed or has trouble paying attention in school may benefit from a "diet" that adds deep pressure or proprioceptive input to help calm the nervous system. Helping the teacher with chores that allow the child to get up and move around, wearing clothing that has sandbags strategically located in pockets, sitting on an inflated seat cushion, or having toys to fidget and squeeze are strategies that may help this child to attend.

Once sensory input has been modulated, it must be understood. The brain must learn to discriminate a red image from a yellow one, a dog's bark from a cat's meow, warm water from cold water, sweet from sour tastes, and a heavy load from a light one. In many cases, input from multiple sensory receptors combine to help the child learn a concept. For example, in learning the difference between running with fast movement versus running with slow movement, the child benefits from a combination of vestibular, proprioceptive, and visual feedback from the activity. Fast movement causes the fluid in the semicircular canals to flow differently than during slow movement, thus causing a different type of vestibular input. At the same time, running fast requires stronger contractions of certain muscles than running slow, creating a different type of proprioceptive input. Finally, as we are running, we see objects in the environment changing their position in relation to our body. If we run fast, they move more quickly than if we run slowly, a difference in visual input.

Therapists using sensorimotor approaches to therapy appreciate the complex interactions between the various sensory modalities, and attempt to modify multiple variables in order to create an environment that is most likely to support motor development.

The importance of motivation and practice

Typically developing children are born with an inner drive to master their bodies and their environment. The infant tries over and over again to grasp that first piece of cereal until he or she finally learns to pinch it precisely between the tips of the thumb and index finger, then plunge it into the mouth with a great sense of triumph. Similarly, the toddler has an almost magnetic attraction to anything that suggests "climb me" in an effort to challenge his or her balance skills and strength. When developmental processes are normal, this inner drive generates considerable repetition and practice of skills, and results in a great deal of positive feedback for the child. Not only does he or she receive the satisfaction that comes from self accomplishment, but the behavior is usually well rewarded by approving parents and caregivers.

Unfortunately, there are a number of reasons why children with developmental coordination disorders may lack the inner drive to explore their environment and to challenge their own development. For one thing, some children who have perceptual differences may not receive the appropriate feedback from their senses to help guide their movement and behavior. The feedback received may be more confusing than helpful, and can sometimes be downright uncomfortable. If you have ever been in a funhouse where curved mirrors and moving floor surfaces are designed to confuse you as you navigate your way through a maze, you have some idea of how the child with sensory processing difficulties might feel. Children with sensory or perceptual differences may present as underactive and passive if they are avoiding challenging circumstances, or as overactive and disorganized if they seek out but do not learn from challenges.

Another problem is that children with coordination problems or developmental delays are commonly teased or victimized by their peers, which naturally leads to reluctant participation in any activity that will draw attention to their shortcomings. Sadly, many well-intentioned parents also draw negative attention to their child's limitations. In an effort to be helpful, the concerned parent may fall into a pattern of constantly asking the child to try harder, to pay better attention, or to watch more closely. Children exposed to this type of interaction may feel as though it is impossible to please their parents, and may quickly develop patterns of low self esteem and a poor tolerance for frustration.

It is extremely important to identify appropriate methods for motivating the child to practice motor skills. Perhaps the best strategy is to embed the practice within an activity that is particularly meaningful for the child. For example, the child who has difficulty manipulating very small objects may vehemently oppose any game involving pegboards or construction toys, but may be thrilled at the idea of decorating cupcakes with small bits of candy or raisins, especially if allowed to eat the end-product. The child who struggles in the morning with the daunting task of getting his or her clothes on, in the right orientation, and with buttons and snaps correctly aligned, might find it far more motivating to practice similar skills during a "dress-up" play activity. Or, the child who is having trouble with handwriting might actually enjoy writing out the family's weekly supermarket list if he is allowed to add one or two favorite menu items of his own choosing.

Another very important concept is to provide the child with frequent positive feedback for his or her efforts. It is important to be consistent, honest, and sincere in offering praise, and to focus on the behavior of the child more than the quality of the performance. Avoid the temptation of exclaiming "Good job!" or "That was terrific!" if it really was not a good job or terrific. The child will recognize your insincerity, despite your good intentions. Comments like "I can see you were paying really close attention that time" or "I like the way you tried doing it more slowly" offer specific and honest feedback as to what the child did right and make it more likely that he or she will repeat the effort. If the child fails a task, it is important to stay calm, acknowledge the failure, but help the child figure out a different way to approach the task. Comments like "Let me see that again—I wonder if it would work better if you…" help to model a problem-solving approach and convey a sense of partnership with the child.

For some children, a more tangible form of reward, such as a star chart, stickers, or access to a favorite activity, can be helpful in motivating the necessary practice. Often, such tangible reward systems also help to take the child's mind off his or her frustration with the task. The use of positive reinforcement approaches will be discussed later in this chapter.

When to teach compensation

Although therapists strive to correct the underlying causes for motor delay or clumsiness, there are times when the gap between a child's ability level and his or her need to accomplish a particular task are too great to wait for therapy or maturation to resolve the problem. Some people believe that it is wrong to teach the child using compensatory strategies, because they are "artificial" and do not really contribute to further developmental maturation. On the contrary, when used judiciously, compensatory strategies can be an important tool for helping the child avoid frustration, experience success, and have sufficient motivation to want to continue learning.

There are as many strategies as there are creative ideas, but most therapists think of compensation as involving a modification either of the amount of assistance provided, or of the tools used. For example, let us consider a second-grade student who has significant motor delays but who wants very badly to learn to tie his shoes because all of his other classmates know how. Depending on this child's specific learning strengths and weaknesses, a variety of compensations might be considered. An example of changing the amount of assistance provided would be for the therapist to create a series of pictures that depict each stage of the sequence involved in tying a bow, serving as a memory aid. These pictures could be inconspicuously posted in the child's locker or cubby, or anyplace else where the shoes might be donned. An example of changing the tools might involve replacing the laces with thick, textured laces, one red and one blue. This might make the laces easier to handle, and provides a visual cue as to which lace goes where. Or, the child could be provided with elastic laces that have already been tied, so he can easily slip the shoes on and off without undoing the bow.

Compensatory strategies are often used for children who have difficulty writing, but who have good language and ideas to express. Although these children still need to work on developing handwriting skills, there are times when it is important to decrease the mental effort involved in the act of writing so the child can more fully express his or her ideas. Use of a scribe who can write down what the child says, allowing verbal responses to test questions, or using various types of word-processing programs may be helpful for these children.

When considered necessary, the therapist may recommend assistive technology to help the child to compensate for his or her motor limitations. Assistive technology refers to any tool or device that offers a child independence in some aspect of self care that he or she cannot perform without help. Assistive technology may be very simple (low-tech) or very complicated (high-tech). Examples of low-tech assistive technology might include using velcro closures instead of buttons to promote dressing independence, or a specially modified pencil to improve the child's grip. An example of high-tech assistive technology might include a voice-activated computer input device for the child who is unable to learn to type. High-tech devices are most commonly recommended for children with severe motoric limitations, while low-tech devices are commonly used for children with DCD. Although some parents find it tempting to look for as many "gadgets" as possible to make their child's life easier, assistive technology should be conservatively used. Negative aspects of assistive technology to consider include cost, the fact that they may draw attention to the disability, and the inconvenience of having to carry the device wherever needed.

Managing problem behaviors

Almost all children, including those with typical development, demonstrate at least occasional patterns of behavior that cause alarm to their parents and teachers. Everyone knows the two-year-old who says "no" to everything, and the pre-schooler who has embarrassing tantrums, often in public places, in an effort to assert his or her independence. However, children with developmental disabilities or delays are somewhat more prone to behavior problems, and these problems may be more prolonged than in typical development if not managed with consistency and sensitivity. It is important to remember that children with developmental differences are particularly susceptible to low self esteem because of their difficulties, and this can lead to such common problems as extreme frustration, task or social avoidance, and passive aggressive behaviors designed to manipulate persons or situations in an effort to avoid failure. Children with serious behavior problems—such as those that put the child or others at risk or under significant stress, those that cause serious social implications, or those that fail to respond to a more generalized approach to management—should be referred to a specialist for behavioral therapy. A variety of professionals, including some pediatricians, psychologists, psychiatrists, social workers, or other counselors, might perform more formal behavior therapy, which may, in some cases, include the use of medication. However, many behavior problems resolve given a more traditional behavior management approach that can be conducted by therapists, teachers, or parents.

Basic behavior management techniques start by identifying the specific behaviors that need to change. It is important to recognize that behavior management will not change the underlying personality characteristics of the child, but may prevent those characteristics from interfering with function in highly select circumstances. For example, the child who is innately fidgety can be expected to remain fidgety even as he or she matures. However, if the fidgeting causes the child to fall from the chair while sitting in the classroom, behavior management techniques might prove successful to prevent fidgeting in the chair during the short period of time that the child needs to attend to a lesson. Similarly, the child who has a low self image and who stubbornly avoids challenging motor tasks can be helped to participate willingly in one or more selected activities, but is likely to remain insecure of his or her abilities until much time has passed and many successes have occurred.

The basic principle behind behavior management strategies is to use consistent, positive rewards for desirable behaviors, and to discourage undesirable behaviors primarily through use of selected inattention. Examples of types of positive rewards might include verbal praise, sticker or star charts, or token rewards that can be used to "purchase" a privilege such as watching a favorite television program. Examples of ways to provide selective inattention include ignoring inappropriate verbal outbursts or clowning behaviors, or using a "time out" chair. Because most children interact with multiple caregivers in the course of a day, it is important for everyone involved with the child (parents, teachers, extended family, etc.) to be in agreement about which behaviors need to change, and which specific rewards or strategies will be used to reach the behavioral goals set for the child. Appendix II includes references for books that can offer guidance on developing positive behavior plans in children. Some general suggestions for managing difficult behavior include the following:

- Praise, praise, praise! It is widely known that positive reinforcement is the best way to teach children to behave, so find every opportunity to "catch them being good" and immediately praise the behavior. When two or more children are together, finding an opportunity to praise one child can motivate the other to imitate the behavior. Reserve scolding or other forms of negative reinforcement for serious behavioral problems. For minor problems, it is better to ignore the behavior until it stops briefly, then immediately praise the behavior you like to see.

- Make a concerted effort to understand the child's particular strengths and weaknesses, to set realistic expectations for the child, and to understand that some types of behavior may be out of his or her control. For example, the child who has poor balance skills may be appropriately fearful when trying to climb a crowded jungle gym, and may strike out at other children who are perceived as a threat to his or her security. It is best to avoid putting the child into situations where such behavior difficulties are likely to occur.

- Always demonstrate a positive, caring attitude towards the child, even if his or her behavior is less than endearing. If you become too upset to maintain a calm approach, its time to end the activity, wait until the situation de-escalates, then discuss the problem afterwards during a more neutral moment.

- Create consistent schedules and routines for those daily activities that have been observed to trigger problem behaviors. Many children with sensory perceptual difficulties find it hard to cope with unpredictable circumstances, and can learn to behave more easily when they can anticipate exactly what is expected of them.

- Be sure that you state your expectations clearly and in terms the child will understand. "Put your crayons away neatly" may be too vague an instruction for the child who does not really understand the concept of "neatness." "Put your crayons away with all the points facing up so you can close the lid" is much more specific. Immediately praise the child's good efforts at following your requests with comments such as "I like the way you put them in the box gently so they won't break."

- Be consistent in your responses to the child's behavior. Find as many opportunities as you can to praise the child's efforts. On the other hand, do not offer praise unless it is truly earned. Be consistent about exhibiting your disapproval of undesirable behaviors. If you expect your child to put away his dirty clothes in the hamper, expect him to comply every night, with no exceptions even if he is tired or it is past bedtime. Do not promise rewards you cannot deliver, and deliver all rewards immediately after they are earned.

- Do not offer choices unless you are prepared to let the child make a choice. For example, if you ask "Are you ready for your bath?" when you really mean "It's bathtime now!," the child may take advantage of a good opportunity to avoid an undesired task. It is far better to find appropriate ways for the child to make choices that allow independence. For example, the child might be allowed to select a bath versus a shower, bar soap versus a bubble bath, or choose which toy to take into the bath. If you do find yourself in a compromising situation, it is usually best to uphold your end of the bargain, as long as the consequences are not serious. In the example above, the child who insists he is not ready for his bath might go to bed dirty, but have to wake up early to bathe before school.

Specialized therapy approaches

There are a number of specialized approaches to therapy for children with DCD that are commonly practiced by occupational and physical therapists, as well as others who work with children with special needs. The most popular of these approaches are *sensory integration therapy* and *neurodevelopmental therapy*. Physical and occupational therapists are taught basic principles of these approaches in their professional training; however, it takes advanced post-professional training, usually including some supervised clinical experience, to become proficient in their application. Because someone may recommend that your child would benefit from sensory integration therapy or neurodevelopmental therapy, you should understand something about them, and know how to evaluate a therapist's qualifications in these areas.

Sensory integration therapy

Sensory integration therapy (SI) is based on the pioneering work of A. Jean Ayres PhD who was trained both in occupational therapy and psychology (Ayres 1979). This is probably the single most popular approach used by therapists for children with DCD. Sensory integration theory is based on an understanding of sensorimotor learning principles as described earlier.

Signs of sensory integration problems are varied, but may include over- or under-sensitivity to touch or movement, abnormally high or low activity level, poorly organized behavior, difficulty learning new motor tasks despite adequate neuromuscular development, or delays in language development or academic progress despite adequate intelligence. Table 3.2 presents common signs and symptoms of sensory integration dysfunction.

Be careful not to jump to the conclusion that your child has a sensory integrative problem if he or she shows one or two signs of the problem, since most children do. Clinical diagnosis of sensory integration dysfunction is based on looking at patterns of symptoms that have been shown in research to exist more frequently in children with specific developmental problems. It's a little bit like diagnosing a cold: one sneeze does not necessarily mean that the child is ill, but if there are many sneezes, a runny nose, and a cough or sore throat, the picture is pretty clear. When a therapist evaluates a child with possible sensory integrative problems, he or she will use multiple tests or clinical measures to evaluate how different skills cluster.

Table 3.2 Signs of possible sensory integrative disorder

Category	Areas of concern
Medical history	Pre- or- perinatal complications
	Feeding difficulties
	Sleep difficulties
	Allergies
	Chronic ear infections
Physical characteristics	Low or high muscle tone
	Clumsiness
	Balance difficulties
	Drooling, poor articulation
Developmental characteristics	Uneven development
	Delayed motor milestones
	Delayed or mixed hand preference
	Poor learning in relation to intelligence
Behavioral characteristics	Unusual craving for or sensitivity to touch, taste, sound, movement
	Avoidance of age-appropriate activities
	Disorganized approach to tasks
	Aggressiveness or acting out
	Poor social interactions with peers
Temperamental characteristics	Distractibility, overactivity
	Difficulty with transitions
	Unusual phobias or compulsions
	Dramatic mood swings

Therapy programs incorporating sensory integration approaches commonly involve one or two sessions per week for a period of at least six months, although the recommended frequency and duration will vary from child to child. After evaluating how the child responds to different sensory inputs, different motoric challenges, and different aspects of social interaction, the therapist designs a learning environment that teaches to the child's strengths. An important part of the therapy is understanding the profound influence that different types of sensory input have on a child's behavior and learning, then modifying the sensory environment so that the child gets exactly what he or she needs in order to learn. For example, a child who is oversensitive to touch may be irritable and distractible, and may avoid activities or situations that include a lot of tactile input, such as using the hands for "messy" play like finger painting. Treatment for this problem might start by involving the child in activity that produces an overall calming effect to reduce the distractibility. Firm touch, slow rocking, and soft rhythmic music are examples of sensory input that might be calming. Next, the therapist might introduce games that gradually encourage the child to accept tactile input, such as reaching in a bowl filled with rice or sand to find favorite toys that have been buried, and to identify them by touch. The therapist will also teach parents and other caregivers how to recognize situations that the child finds disorganizing, so that you can modify the situation. For example, if your child's school expects everyone to finger paint, there might be ways to make this activity more comfortable for your child such as changing the temperature or the texture of the paint.

It is important to recognize that sensory integration therapy is a controversial method that some doctors do not recommend, although research suggests that it is effective for some children. It is wise to obtain an evaluation by a therapist with special training in sensory integration before considering this approach as an option. Certification in one assessment battery, the Sensory Integration and Praxis Tests (SIPT), is available to therapists through two separate organizations. Sensory Integration International (SII), listed in Appendix III at the end of this book, is one of these organizations. It also maintains a registry of certified therapists and can provide recommendations as to the availability of certified therapists within a given geographic region. More recently, the University of Southern California, in collaboration with Western Psychological Services (also listed in the appendices), has provided training programs as well. However, you should be aware that the SIPT is not an appropriate test for all children, and that certification does not tell you anything about the therapist's actual experience or skill in providing treatment. When selecting a therapist, look for someone who has certification plus other continuing education in the approach, and who has received supervision in clinical practice with children who have similar problems.

Neurodevelopmental therapy

Neurodevelopmental therapy (NDT) is a treatment approach based on the work of Berta Bobath, a physical therapist, and her husband Dr Karel Bobath, and is one of the most widely used developmental approaches to motor learning (Bigsby 2003; Bobath and Bobath 1984; Howle 2002). It is sometimes referred to as the Bobath approach, and is most widely used by physical, occupational, and speech therapists in the treatment of children with cerebral palsy or other forms of neuromuscular dysfunction affecting muscle tone, although it also has application with children whose motor impairment is more mild.

Muscle tone refers to the amount of tension present in a muscle. You may know that children with serious brain damage such as cerebral palsy tend to have either too much muscle tone (spasticity), too little tone (hypotonia or floppiness), or fluctuating tone. Some children with DCD also have abnormalities of muscle tone, although it is usually to a much lesser extent. For reasons we do not fully understand, it is particularly common for children with developmental coordination disorders to have low muscle tone, sometimes referred to as *hypotonia*. Therapists evaluate muscle tone by feeling the muscles, moving the limbs through their range of motion, and observing the child as he or she moves from one position to another. The determination of hypotonia is somewhat subjective, and is considered significant only if it interferes with the quality of the child's movement in such a way as to disrupt the development of functional skills. However, there are several fairly easy signs of low muscle tone that can be observed by anyone, and might suggest the need to seek the opinion of a professional. Table 3.3 suggests possible signs of hypotonia.

Table 3.3 Signs that may suggest hypotonia

In infant or toddler:

- Feels floppy, like a "sack of potatoes" when held
- Muscles feel unusually mushy or soft
- Has weak suck, takes longer than average to feed, or fatigues easily and needs to rest
- Often leaves mouth open, tongue hanging out, excessive drooling
- Demonstrates delays in developmental milestones (sitting, crawling, standing)
- Tends to be physically passive, explores environment less than peers

In older child:

- Poor posture in sitting or standing
- Seems to tire easily during physical play
- Some joints (especially elbows and fingers) are excessively flexible, bend back easily
- Eats with mouth open, may drool or lose food from mouth
- May have trouble making some speech sounds (poor articulation)
- Holds tools tightly, uses excessive pressure when drawing, cutting

Abnormal muscle tone can have a significant influence over the child's ability to develop balance, to move from one position to another, and to develop a sense of security and control over the body. The child with abnormal muscle tone tends to get "stuck" in body positions and movement patterns that feel safe, but that make it hard to move from one position to another. To get a sense of how this might feel to the child, try the following experiment. Imagine that you have low muscle tone in the trunk, causing you to sit at a desk with a slouching posture or rounded back.

Notice that when your back is rounded, if you want to look up, let's say at a computer terminal or a whiteboard, you will tend to overextend the neck muscles so that the head rests back on the shoulders. Now try to move your arms around, as though to write on a paper, move a mouse, or reach towards a computer screen. You will probably notice that the position of your body causes some degree of tension in the muscles of the neck, shoulder, and upper back, limiting their freedom of movement. For a child working under these uncomfortable circumstances, it may be very hard to concentrate effectively on the task at hand. Also, as you have learned, motor development heavily depends on sensory feedback from the body. When movement patterns are abnormal, the sensory feedback from that movement is also abnormal, so the child learns to continue using those abnormal movements. In standing, the child may tilt the hips forward to let the spine carry the body's weight. This causes the lower back to curve inwards (kyphosis), and the shoulders to curve forward, as illustrated in Figure 3.2.

Figure 3.2 Typical posture of a child with low muscle tone

In this position, it is hard for the child to shift weight smoothly from one leg to the other, or to move with rotation around the spine.

Children with hypotonia may also exhibit excessive flexibility of the joints, what lay persons sometimes think of as "double jointedness." This is easiest to observe in the elbows and finger joints. When children have low muscle tone affecting the arms and hands, they tend to hold a pencil or other tools using inefficient body mechanics, and often with excessive force. Figure 3.3 illustrates one typical pattern for holding a pencil that is often used by children with hypotonia.

Figure 3.3 Typical pencil grasp of a child with low muscle tone

The wrist is flexed (bent forward) instead of in a neutral or slightly extended (bent back) position, and the thumb is pressed tightly against the pencil shaft instead of opposing the shaft to form an "O." The child using this grip may press down very hard on the paper, and may have trouble moving the arm smoothly across the page to write a sentence. When the pencil is held in this manner, the child is unable to use small movements of the fingertips to make letter strokes. Instead, movement comes from the elbow and shoulder, which is far less precise, and much more fatiguing to the child.

Therapists using NDT principles focus on teaching parents and other caregivers how to position, carry, and handle the child during routine daily activities in a way that encourages more normal muscle tone. This enhances the child's opportunity to experience the sensation of normal movement and learn from it. Parents who opt for therapy using an NDT approach should expect that they will be required to learn a variety of handling techniques that they should incorporate whenever possible during the child's typical daily activities.

Therapists are taught basic NDT principles in school, but become competent in the techniques through additional training and practical experiences after they have graduated. Therapists may become certified in basic pediatric NDT procedures by taking an eight-week course sponsored by the Neuro-developmental Treatment Association (NDTA). This organization also maintains a registry of certified therapists, and is included in Appendix III.

Other approaches

Many educationally based programs address some aspects of motor skills development through physical education curricula and handwriting training programs that are designed for all students. For children with more specific problems, sensory integration therapy and neurodevelopmental therapy are among the most common approaches used by therapists, yet there are many other approaches that are less widely known or accepted. *Complementary and alternative medicine* (CAM) is a term that refers to a diverse array of healthcare systems, practices, and interventions that are considered to be outside the realm of conventional medicine. Some of these approaches have achieved popularity among consumers, but in general there is limited research to assure that the methods are effective and safe. It is always helpful for parents and professionals to be aware of the variety of options available for intervention, but they should proceed cautiously when considering a more controversial approach. It is easy to become excited about a new therapy that shows promise, but remember that more therapy is not necessarily better therapy, and that every intervention carries costs in the form of out-of-pocket expenses, time, mental effort, and disappointment if the treatment fails to be helpful.

It is easy for parents and professionals alike to be fooled into thinking an intervention "works" when there are anecdotal success stories or media attention, but remember that the *placebo effect* may account for some of the success stories. The placebo effect refers to the perception that an intervention leads to improved outcomes when, in fact, there could be other factors that have led to the outcome. Remember that, with any intervention, a professional enters into a relationship with the child and family, offers helpful advice and emotional support, and may be able to help the child to improve his or her skills through this positive relationship. Improvement may or may not relate to the intervention per se, which is why conventional medicine looks for interventions that have undergone rigorous scientific study to prove effectiveness. This does not mean that you should exclude the possibility of using alternative approaches, just that you should proceed with caution.

If you do choose to pursue an alternative or complementary approach, it is important to understand what training is necessary to assure competency in the technique, and to know what is and is not covered by insurance or other sources of funding. Discuss the intervention with other professionals involved with the child so that they can offer their perspectives and advise as to the potential for any adverse effects. Some alternative interventions are described in Table 3.4, which also suggests where to obtain further information about the method.

Choosing the best intervention

In practice, most good therapists know that no one single approach works best, and that techniques from a variety of approaches must be skillfully combined to help each child overcome his or her unique problems. It is the ability to practice therapy holistically, drawing from many frames of reference and many techniques, while staying focused on achieving goals that are important to the child and family, that makes a therapist truly skilled.

Table 3.4 Examples of alternative therapy approaches

Type of therapy	Description	For more information
Aquatic therapy	The use of swimming and other pool activities to promote motor skills. Therapy is usually conducted by an occupational or physical therapist. The reduced gravitational pull provided by an aquatic environment, often combined with use of warm water, makes movement easier for some children.	The Aquatic Exercise Association 201 S. Tamiami Trail, Suite 3 Nokomis, FL 34275 Tel: +1 (888) 232-9283 www.aeawave.com International Council for Aquatic Therapy and Rehabilitation Industry Certification 2829 S. Manito Boulevard Spokane, WA 99203-2542 Tel: +1 (425) 444-2720 www.icatric.org
Aromatherapy	The selected use of essential plant oils applied through inhalation, diffusion, or massage used to improve health and well-being. Most oils have stimulating, sedative, regulating, or euphoric effects, and may help to reduce stress and promote regulation among children with autism or other learning disabilities.	National Association for Holistic Aromatherapy 3327 W. Indian Trail Road PMB 144 Spokane, WA 99208 Tel: +1 (508) 325-3419 www.naha.org
Auditory training	The use of sound stimulation, provided through headphones, designed to improve the child's listening, learning, movement, organization, and self esteem. Method used especially with children with sensory processing difficulties including autism and ADHD. Various programs include Berard Auditory Integration Training (AIT), the Tomatis Method, and the Listening Program.	The Berard AIT Website: www.berardaitwebsite.com The Tomatis Method: www.tomatis.com The Listening Program: www.advancedbrain.com

Continued on next page

Table 3.4 continued

Type of therapy	Description	For more information
Brain Gym	A program of physical movements designed to integrate body and mind to improve concentration, memory, reading and writing skills, organization, listening, and physical coordination. The exercises focus on crossing the midline, lengthening activities, and energy exercises.	Brain Gym International The Educational Kinesiology Foundation 1575 Spinnaker Drive, Suite 204 B Ventura, CA Tel: +1 (800) 356-2109 www.BrainGym.org
Craniosacral therapy	A manual therapy approach that focuses on releasing pressure or binding of the membranes and fluid surrounding the brain and spinal cord. Proponents believe this allows for greater flexibility and posture, reduces the effects of stress, enhances health, and improves resistance to disease.	The Upledger Institute, Inc. 11211 Prosperity Farms Road, D325 Palm Beach Gardens, FL 33410 Tel: +1 (561) 622-4334 www.upledger.com The Upledger Institute UK 2 Marshall Place Perth PH2 8AH, UK Tel: +44 (0)1738 444404 www.upledger.co.uk
Dance/movement therapy	The use of movement as a psychotherapeutic process to further the emotional, cognitive, and physical integration of the individual, and for purposes related to disease prevention and health promotion. Therapists complete a Master's degree in dance/movement therapy, supervised internship, and national registration.	The American Dance Therapy Association, Inc. 2000 Century Plaza, Suite 108 10632 Little Patuxent Parkway Columbia, MD 21044 Tel: +1 (410) 997-4048 www.adta.org The Association for Dance Movement Therapy UK 32 Meadfoot Lane Torquay TQ1 2BW, UK www.admt.org.uk

Type of therapy	Description	For more information
Developmental optometry	The use of special lenses, vision exercises, and other vision training methods to alleviate inadequate visual skills and visual stress. These vision problems may cause a variety of functional problems, including incoordination in sports. Practice of developmental optometry requires postgraduate training beyond that required to practice general optometry.	Optometric Extension Program Foundation, Inc. 1921 E. Carnegie Avenue, Ste.3-L Santa Ana, CA 92705-5510 Tel: +1 (714) 250-8070 www.oep.org College of Optometrists in Vision Development 243 N. Lindbergh Boulevard, Suite 310 St. Louis, MO 63141 Tel: +1 (888) 268-3770 www.covd.org
Interactive Metronome	A three- to five-week computer-driven program that combines a musical metronome with interactive hand and foot exercises that challenge a person's rhythm and timing to improve foundation skills important to learning and development. Improvements are expected in attention, motor control and coordination, language processing, reading and math fluency, and ability to regulate impulsivity.	Interactive Metronome 2500 Weston Road, Suite 403 Weston, FL 33331 Tel: +1 (877) 994-6776 www.interactivemetronome.com
Myofascial release	A therapeutic treatment using gentle, manual manipulation of fascia, which is a tough connective tissue occurring throughout the body, in order to promote health and improved posture.	Myofascial Release Treatment Centers Suite 100, 222 West Lancaster Avenue Paoli, PA 10301 Tel: +1 (610) 644-0136 www.myofascialrelease.com

Continued on next page

Table 3.4 continued

Type of therapy	Description	For more information
Therapeutic brushing (Wilbarger Protocol)	A specific program of brushing the child in order to reduce the effects of sensory defensiveness, which may include overactivity, inattentiveness, and emotional volatility. The procedure is based on principles of sensory integration therapy, and has become a popular adjunct to many occupational therapy programs.	Several publications available through: PDP Products 14524 61st Street Ct. N. Stillwater, MN 55082 Tel: +1 (651) 439-8865 www.pdppro.com
Therapeutic massage	The use of various massage techniques to promote physical, emotional and intellectual development of the child, and to improve bonding and attachment between the child and parent.	American Massage Therapy Association 500 Davis Street Evanston, IL 60201 Tel: +1 (847) 905-2700 www.amtamassage.org British Massage Therapy Council 17 Rymers Lane Oxon OX4 3JU, UK Tel: +44 (0)1865 774123
Therapeutic riding (hippotherapy)	The use of horse and equine-oriented activities to achieve a variety of therapeutic goals, including cognitive, physical, emotional, social, educational and behavioral goals. Hippotherapy is a specific type of therapeutic riding that is based on a medical model, and is practiced by occupational and physical therapists who have special training in this method.	North American Riding for the Handicapped Association P.O. Box 33150 Denver, CO 80233 Tel: +1 (800) 369-7433 www.narha.org Riding for the Disabled Association Lavinia Norfolk House Avenue R Stonleigh Park Warwickshire CV8 2LY, UK Tel: +44 (0)845 658 1082 www.riding-for-disabled.org.uk

Type of therapy	Description	For more information
Yoga	Yoga uses an integrated series of balanced poses to increase body awareness, strength, and flexibility. These are combined with specialized breathing exercises and relaxation techniques that may improve concentration and reduce hyperactivity.	Yoga for the Special Child 2100 Constitution Boulevard, Suite 103 Sarasota, FL 34231 Tel: +1 (888) 900-YOGA www.specialyoga.com The Special Yoga Centre The Tay Building 2a Wrentham Avenue London NW10 3HA, UK Tel: +44 (0)208 968 1900 www.specialyoga.org.uk

In deciding which approach they will use, therapists must consider a number of factors. Sometimes, the child's clinical profile provides strong clues as to the method or methods that are likely to be most effective with his or her unique set of problems. For example, we might predict that a child with significantly high or low muscle tone will respond best to a neurodevelopmental approach, while a child who is extremely oversensitive to sensory input, and, as a result, avoids many play situations, might respond better to sensory integration therapy. Sometimes, the personal interests expressed by the child and his or her family may suggest the appropriateness of an alternative approach. The child who has balance and postural control difficulties and who is passionate about animals may respond more effectively to therapeutic horseback riding than a child who is more cautious and fearful around animals. The family who has a home swimming pool may be able to provide home carry-over of strategies learned through aquatic therapy more easily than the family who has to travel to the local public swimming pool.

The therapist must also consider his or her own training with different methodologies, and will probably show a bias towards those methods with which he or she has had the most training and clinical experience. In addition, therapists must unfortunately take into consideration any external limits to their ability to select the treatment approaches that they consider to be ideal. For example, some interventions require significant home carry-over by parents to be effective. This may be fine for some families, but if the family consists of a single working mother who has limited time and energy after work, and who is uncomfortable assuming the role of "therapist," it may be necessary to reconsider the approach. Insurance companies may be unwilling to pay for the extended duration of therapy needed for some developmental approaches, requiring the therapist to focus more on helping the child and family to quickly develop compensatory approaches to functional problems. In school settings, therapists may lack access to the special equipment needed to provide therapy in the same way it can be delivered in a private clinic. They are also limited to providing therapy that addresses educationally related goals, and may be unable to address functional limitations that do not impact the child's performance in school. For many children, choosing a "best approach" to therapy requires thoughtful consideration and, sometimes, trials in different approaches.

References

Ayres, A.J. (1979) *Sensory Integration and the Child*. Los Angeles, CA: Western Psychological Services.

Bigsby, R. (2003) "Developmental and neurological perspectives." In E.B. Crepeau, E.S. Cohn and B.A.B. Schell (eds) *Willard and Spackman's Occupational Therapy (10th Edition)*, pp.243–252. Philadelphia, PA: Lippincott, Williams and Wilkins.

Bobath, K. and Bobath, B (1984) "Neuro-Developmental Treatment." In D. Scrutton (ed.) *Management of the Motor Disorders of Children with Cerebral Palsy: Clinics in Developmental Medicine,* No. 90, pp.6–18. Philadelphia, PA: J.B. Lippincott.

Howle, J.M. (ed.) (2002) *Neuro-Developmental Treatment Approach: Theoretical Foundations and Principles of Clinical Practice*. Laguna Beach, CA: NDTA.

Part II

PRACTICAL STRATEGIES AND ACTIVITIES FOR HOME AND SCHOOL

Chapter 4

PROMOTING
BASIC MOTOR SKILLS

This chapter will discuss specific strategies that may be used by parents, teachers, or therapists in helping the child with coordination difficulties to develop better motor skills and to become more successful in various aspects of daily life. In developing a program of activities, several broad considerations are important to bear in mind:

- Both you and the child should be clear about your goals for the intervention, as this will help you to keep focused on the important aspects of learning. The clumsy child is not likely to "outgrow" his or her clumsiness, but can learn to be successful with skills and activities that are important in daily life, and can be helped to develop a more positive attitude and enthusiasm for physically challenging activities. For the younger child, goals may be stated very simply, for example "We are going to be playing games and doing exercises that will help your hands to be stronger. That will make it easier for you to learn to write and to use scissors." The older child may be engaged in setting personal goals, such as participating in a desired sport, learning to ride a bike, or completing written homework without having his or her hand "get tired." As you plan activities, refer back to these goals so the child is clear that there is a purpose to the activity. Remember that your goals may not be exactly the same as the child's goals, and remember to set new goals periodically as the child gains greater and greater success.

- Given the complexities of juggling work responsibilities, managing a household, caring for other children, and maintaining a personal life, it is not surprising that parents frequently struggle with finding time to work one-on-one with their child. It is important to understand that the amount of time spent in engaging the child in an activity program is less important than the quality of the time. If you can, try to find several times each week to work on specific skills and activities, varying the activities so that the child maintains high interest and cooperation. You will also find that many helpful activities can be embedded within daily routines. For example, the child who needs to work on developing a stronger pinch grasp might help out in the kitchen by tearing lettuce or snapping green beans.

- Practice in motor or other skills should always occur in a positive atmosphere and with appropriate incentives. For most children, genuine and heartfelt praise is sufficient to motivate effort. Others may require more tangible rewards, such as a star chart, sticker, or earned privilege. Remember to be very precise in the feedback you give, as it will serve not only as a reward but as a teaching tool. "Nice try!" is less helpful than "I really like the way you kept your eye on the ball the whole time it was coming towards you," or "I can see that you were resting your arm against the table to help keep your hand steady." If the frustration level of either you or your child is such that you cannot have fun when working on skill development, it is time to seek the help of a professional who can help you and your child to develop a more positive working relationship. Do not let yourself feel guilty or inadequate if a professional has more success than you do in engaging the cooperation of your child, as this is perfectly normal. Instead, ask to participate actively in therapy sessions so you can observe and attempt to imitate the therapist's strategies and routines.

If your child receives therapy or has had a formal evaluation of motor skills, you may seek advice from a professional as to exactly what areas of motor development are important to reinforce. There are several broad areas of motor skill development that are likely to be helpful for most children. These include: body awareness, motor planning, bilateral motor integration, balance skills, and fine motor control. Promoting skills in the areas of functional vision and oral-motor coordination will be helpful for those children who experience issues in these more discrete areas of motor difficulty.

Body awareness

Body awareness refers to the unconscious sense of body position, movement and force that comes from special sensory receptors located in the joints and muscles. It is the sense that tells us what position our arms and legs are in even if our eyes are closed. This sense is also called proprioception. When the sense of proprioception is functioning effectively, it allows the child to make automatic, continual, unconscious adjustments to body positions and movements according to the demands of a task. For example, during a coloring activity, the child automatically changes the direction of strokes to stay within the lines, and grades the pressure on the crayon to get just the right shade of color. The eyes tell the child whether the effort is working; there is very little, if any, thought as to how the hand *feels* as it makes these adjustments. When the sense of proprioception does not work effectively, the child may have to pay conscious attention to things that should happen automatically. For example, in playing "Simon says," the child may actually have to look at his or her body parts to make sure that directions were followed correctly.

Children with low muscle tone seem particularly susceptible to having problems with proprioception. Children with low muscle tone also tend to have poor core trunk strength. This relates to the ability of the middle part of the body — the trunk — to support posture against gravity, to maintain balance, and to create a strong and stable base allowing the arms and legs to move independently with strength and power. Children with this problem benefit from activities that focus on strengthening the muscles, bearing weight on the arms, pushing and pulling, providing firm touch, and working against resistance. Simple exercises to build core trunk strength are illustrated in Table 4.1.

The use of proprioceptive activities is also often helpful for children with attention or organizational problems, as the added input may produce a calming effect. The following types of activities provide strong proprioceptive input:

- Back rubs or massages.

- Wearing tight, elastic clothes such as stretch pants.

- Helping with "heavy work" activities around the house, such as carrying in groceries from the car, pushing a wheelbarrow in the garden, rolling out thick cookie dough.

- Tug of war.

- Perform "wall push-ups" by placing arms against a wall and pushing in and out.

- Providing extra proprioceptive input when learning a new motor skill. For example, press the child's palms together and firmly apply pressure to help them "get ready" to write. Or, press down gently on the child's hips when he or she is trying to learn to balance on an unstable surface.

- Push-ups, sit-ups, chin-ups.

- Crawling, bear-walking, crab-walking through an obstacle course.

- Jump rope, jumping jacks, jumping on a trampoline, pogo stick.

- Pulling another child on a wagon or other riding toy.

- Make a child "sandwich" by squeezing between two sofa cushions (the "bread") and then rubbing on various "ingredients" such as cheese, mustard, relish.

- Shoveling snow, raking leaves.

- Playing with stiff clay or dough.

- Chewing resistive foods, such as gum, caramels, gummy bears, fruit leather, licorice, or crunchy foods such as chips or pretzels.

Table 4.1 Simple exercises to develop core trunk strength

The "Superman" exercise

Lie on your tummy and hold arms and legs off the floor to try to fly like "superman." Try to hold the position for 30 seconds.

The "Rocking Chair" exercise

Lie on your back with your arms around your knees and rock gently back and forth without letting go of your legs or kicking your feet.

The "Wheelbarrow" exercise

Walk on your hands while someone holds your ankles.

The "Statue" exercise

In a crawling position, hold one or two arms or legs off the floor and be "stiff like a statue." Another person pushes gently against the hips or shoulder to try to "break" the statue.

The "Sledding" exercise

Sit on a carpet square or piece of cardboard placed on a slippery floor. With hands on your head, use your feet to scoot across the floor.

The "Strongman" exercise

Kneel with your hips straight, and push against another person's hands without leaning forward or sitting back on your feet.

The "Letter V" exercise

Lie on your back, then raise your arms and legs straight to make the letter "V." Try putting puppets on your hands and arms to make it fun.

The "Food Wrestling" exercise

Two children sit on the floor facing each other. Put your hands behind you to support your weight, and raise your feet to touch the feet of the other child. Each child pushes against the other's feet.

Motor planning

Motor planning ability, also referred to as praxis, is the ability to conceptualize, plan, and carry out an unfamiliar motor task or motor sequence. It is different from motor coordination, which refers to the ability to control body movements in a smooth manner. In order to motor plan successfully, the child must have a mental picture or idea of what needs to occur, clear vestibular and proprioceptive feedback regarding movement, and the ability to make automatic, reflexive adjustments to moving in time and space. Children with motor planning difficulties (*dyspraxia*) have problems with learning new skills that involve using the body. They tend to require extra practice and reinforcement when learning new motor skills, and do not usually generalize these skills to new situations with ease (for example, tying a bow on shoes is different from tying a hair ribbon). Some children may become so frustrated with any game or activity that challenges motor skill that they avoid these tasks whenever possible. Others may be so unaware of their bodies that when trying to learn something new, they repeat the same movements over and over, even if unsuccessful, and can think of no strategies for trying it a different way. Children with motor planning difficulty tend to be disorganized in their use of time and materials, and often have difficulty displaying independence with simple routines involving household or school responsibilities. Because motor coordination may be normal even in the presence of motor planning difficulties, many children can show surprising skill in performing motor activities that are familiar and well rehearsed. Suggestions for improving motor planning skills are as follows:

- Expect that teaching new skills will require considerable practice and repetition, and may have to be re-taught periodically even after the child seems capable of performing the task.

- Begin a teaching session by first providing sensory experiences that help the child to be more aware of body sensations (see body awareness activities listed in the previous section), or that offer vestibular or tactile sensation. This helps the child to be ready to "listen" to his or her body.

- Many children learn motor skills best using a procedure called "verbal task analysis" in which they are taught to verbalize each step of the process as a reminder to their body. For example, if learning to make a letter "T" the child might be taught to say "I start at the top and make a line going down, then jump up and make a line across the top." This strategy often works best if you also use hand-over-hand assistance, taking the child through the correct motions, at the same time as you teach the verbal cues.

- Add sensory cues, usually tactile or visual, to help the child attend to selected aspects of the task. For example, for the child who forgets to use the non-dominant hand to position or stabilize paper when writing or drawing, you might tap your finger periodically on the back of the hand with an encouraging comment. An example of using visual cues would be to provide writing paper with different colored lines to show where the line placement should be.

- Children with motor planning difficulties almost always have perceptual differences involving their tactile system. Some have difficulties with sensory modulation (see Chapter 3) and benefit from a sensory diet of organizing inputs. Others have difficulty with discrimination of touch inputs. Games or activities that involve tactile discrimination can be very helpful in promoting attention to body cues. Examples include digging in rice, sand or putty to find small hidden objects; guessing textures or shapes with eyes closed; finger painting in shaving cream or textured paint; guessing where he or she is touched lightly with a finger or cotton swab; or guessing a shape or letter of the alphabet drawn on his or her back with your finger.

- Activities that involve imitating body movements or sequences are helpful. Examples include "Simon says" or charades; using various animal walks while going through an obstacle course; learning new dance steps or action songs; or thinking about how many different ways you can do something (how many different ways can you propel a ball toward another person, or how many different ways can you "ride" a carpet square across a linoleum floor).

- Performing activities with the eyes closed can help to increase awareness of the feel of body movements. Try having the child write his or her name on the board with eyes closed. Or have the child go through a simple obstacle course first with eyes open, then with eyes closed.

- Activities that require rapid anticipation of movement also help to teach motor planning. Dodge ball, tether ball, or badminton are examples of such activities.

Bilateral motor integration

Another important area of basic motor skill development is bilateral motor integration. This refers to the progressive ability of the two sides of the body to cooperate with and complement each other in order to successfully complete a variety of motor tasks. It is the aspect of motor development that allows a child to develop a dominant hand for use of skilled tools, and contributes to the child's cognitive awareness of certain spatial concepts, especially of right and left.

Consider the bilateral skill that is involved in an activity such as cutting out a paper doll. The dominant hand grasps the scissors and makes the repetitive opening and closing movements that are involved in cutting. The nondominant hand holds the paper, maintaining it in a position that is perpendicular to the cutting blades, and continually turns and orients the paper as the scissors proceed along the line. Because the eyes are needed to assure that the cutting blades are staying on or near the line, the child must use feedback from the body (proprioception) to make automatic adjustments to the position and orientation of the nondominant hand. As previously mentioned in Chapter 3, bilateral motor integration depends heavily on information from the vestibular system.

Children with difficulties including bilateral motor integration may demonstrate a variety of signs and symptoms. Most noticeable, there may be a delay in determining hand preference for pencil or scissors. Most children will begin to show a preference for one hand or the other by about two and a half years of age. Dominance typically develops gradually, but by the start of kindergarten, most children will use one hand consistently for pencil, crayons, and scissors. Hand switching for less skilled activities, such as playing with construction toys, pointing to pictures in a book, or turning a doorknob, may continue through the school years. It is important for children to have a clear hand preference for skilled tool use by the time they enter kindergarten, because a large part of the school day is spent in fine motor activities that employ these tools. Children who switch hands become confused about certain motor patterns and sequences that need to become automatic and habitual. For example, left-handed children tend to hold their pencil with a slight bend to the wrist and with the paper angled toward the right, as this allows them to see the writing they have just produced before their hand covers it as they write from left to right. Right handers usually hold their pencil with the wrist straight or held slightly back, and angle the paper in the opposite direction. If the child is switching back and forth, he or she will have difficulty learning consistent work habits. Also, it is important to consider that motor skills must be frequently practiced in order to become automatic and well controlled. Children who switch hands receive less practice with each hand than nonswitchers.

Hand switching relates closely to development of the ability to cross the midline of the body. We observe that at age two and a half to three, most children will reach for an object with the hand that is closest to the object. That is, if a toy is placed toward the child's right, he is most likely to reach for it with his or her right hand. If play with the toy involves reaching over to place it more towards the left of the child's midline, he or she is likely to transfer the toy to the left hand before letting it go. By four or five years of age, most children will cross the midline to reach for a skilled tool such as scissors or pencil, but may continue to reach with the closest hand for materials that require less skill to manipulate, such as blocks or puzzle pieces. An easy way to observe for difficulties in crossing the midline of the body is to have the child face you while you assume various postures that he or she must imitate rapidly. Use a variety of postures including some that do and some that do not involve crossing the midline. For example, putting your left hand over your left ear and your right hand on your right knee while you tilt to the right does not require crossing the midline. Putting your left hand over your right ear and your right hand on your left elbow does require crossing the midline. Changing positions quickly and observing the child's ability to imitate can provide good clues about this skill. The following suggestions may be helpful for the child with delays in bilateral motor integration.

To encourage more consistent hand preference

- Use a ribbon, wrist watch, or friendship bracelet to be worn on the preferred hand as a reminder to use that hand when writing or cutting.

- When offering a crayon, pencil, or other skilled tool, offer it toward the child's preferred hand. Either sit facing the child, or on the side closest to his or her preferred side.

- During crafts or other projects, place materials used on the side of the table closest to the preferred hand so the child will not have to reach across his or her midline to obtain desired materials.

- Encourage games where the nondominant hand "holds" a container, and the dominant hand "fills" the container—for example, pushing marbles into a hole cut in the plastic lid of a coffee can, placing pennies into a piggy bank, measuring teaspoons of water to fill a jar, or using tweezers or tongs to fill a basket with cotton puffs.

To develop general bilateral motor integration skills

- Practice games such as "Twister," "Simon says," or other body position imitation games.

- Place a carpet square on a slippery floor (e.g. linoleum) and practice "racing" by paddling with arms and legs using different "patterns" (e.g. sit on the carpet and use both feet to propel; kneel on the carpet and use

both hands to propel; put one foot on the carpet and use the other leg
to propel).

- Practice jumping or hopping games such as hopscotch, leapfrog,
  jumping jacks, cheerleading moves, or jumping to "patterns" on a
  trampoline (e.g. right, right, left, left or right, left, clap, right, left, clap).

- Hold one crepe-paper streamer in each hand and practice various
  bilateral patterns.

- Hold one piece of chalk in each hand. Standing at a blackboard, practice
  drawing shapes, patterns, or letters using both hands at the same time
  with the eyes closed. Encourage the child to try to make the right-hand
  picture look the same as the left-hand picture.

- Lie on the floor and pretend to make "angels in the snow" with eyes
  open and eyes closed. Vary the patterns—for example, moving the right
  arm and left leg while the other limbs remain still.

Balance skills

Balance is another important component of motor skill in the developing child.
Balance skills are based upon input from several sensory modalities. Perhaps of
greatest importance is the vestibular sense, which provides input to the central
nervous system about gravitational pull, motion, and speed. Some children with
inadequate sensory processing of vestibular input may be overly sensitive, causing
them to get dizzy easily and to avoid activities that include strong movement experiences. Children with this sort of problem often show a strong preference for
maintaining their head in a position of vertical alignment with the world, and avoid
such activities as hanging upside down on a monkey bar, performing somersaults,
or lying back on a piece of equipment that rocks or is otherwise unstable. Others
with vestibular difficulties are undersensitive to vestibular input, and may seek out
extra movement experiences in an effort to "fuel" their central nervous system
with meaningful information.

Balance is also highly dependent on proprioceptive feedback. Movement in
any part of the body should result in unconscious, automatic postural adjustments,
often subtle, in other parts of the body. For example, when a right-handed child
writes a sentence on a piece of paper, the hand moves along a path that causes the
body to shift weight and the head to turn slightly toward the right, thus allowing
smooth movement of the arm across the page. These subtle body adjustments are
sometimes referred to as postural background movements, and help the body to
move fluidly and as a whole unit. Visual feedback is also a factor in maintaining

balance. As the body moves, so do the visual images that reach the central nervous system, providing additional cues that the body needs to make adjustments in response to the situation. You may have had the experience of watching a spinning toy or carnival ride, and feeling dizzy as a result. This illustrates the close relationship between the visual and vestibular systems. You may have also learned that fixating on a stable visual target when attempting to balance on one foot may improve your performance. Ballet dancers and figure skaters use this strategy to maintain their balance when learning to stay upright during spins. If the child can balance very significantly better with eyes open than with eyes closed, there is a strong possibility that he or she is overly relying on visual cues to maintain balance, and needs help to develop stronger perceptual awareness of feedback through the vestibular and proprioceptive systems.

In helping the child with these problems to improve their balance skills, it is important to respect the child's tolerance for movement. Children who are undersensitive and who crave movement need guidance and supervision to make sure that they play in ways that are safe, since their body may not provide accurate cues about the risks of injury. Children who are oversensitive may need a great deal of coaxing to participate in movement activities. Start with slow, rhythmic movements and gradually increase the speed and postural demands. Many oversensitive children also respond to use of firm touch or other proprioceptive inputs either prior to, or coinciding with, movement activities. The following are activity suggestions to promote better awareness of vestibular input and to develop balance skills:

- Encourage safe, controlled participation on a variety of playground equipment that incorporates movement: swings, slides, trapeze bars, merry-go-rounds.

- Inexpensive home equipment to consider includes exercise trampolines, sit-n-spin, rocker toys.

- Roughhouse play or piggy back rides provide lots of vestibular and proprioceptive input.

- For the child who has difficulty jumping off the floor with two feet, start by teaching him or her to jump off a low step or platform onto something that will make noise, for example bubble wrap.

- Practice "tightrope walking" a line through a simple obstacle course. Use wide ribbon, long strips of paper, or two-by-four inch pieces of wood to mark the course. Or use carpet squares to mark a path for jumping or hopping.

Fine motor coordination

Fine motor coordination skills are especially important for the young school-aged child, since they spend such a large portion of their day in coloring, pasting, and using manipulative toys and materials. To become successful, the child needs to learn to hold his or her arm and wrist in a stable position while isolating finger movements according to the demands of the particular task.

Developmentally, stability begins at the shoulder, then works its way down the arm to the elbow, then forearm, then wrist. For most fine motor activities, the wrist is held straight or in a slightly extended position (i.e. bent back), as this position helps to provide anatomical balance to the small muscles in the hands and fingers so that the radial side of the hand (closest to the thumb) and the ulnar side of the hand (closest to the pinky finger) can work dynamically together. When in this position, the thumb can easily oppose the other fingers to manipulate small objects with control, and the ring and pinky finger can curl into a position that allows stability of the hand. Try a fine motor activity such as stringing small beads, first with your wrists flexed (bending forward), then slightly extended (bending back), to feel the difference it can make with fine motor control. Children with low muscle tone, so common among children with developmental motor concerns, often have great difficulty developing these patterns of stability. Unfortunately, they are often required or encouraged to learn to use fine motor materials before they are developmentally ready to do so. In response to this, the child may adopt atypical patterns of grasp or tool usage in an effort to compensate for the instability.

In helping the child to develop improved fine motor control two principles are observed. First, it is important to help the child with exercises and activities that develop shoulder, elbow, and wrist stability. Second, the child is engaged in activities that promote speed and ease of movement when using the fingers to manipulate small objects. The following activity suggestions are recommended.

To develop shoulder, elbow, and wrist stability

- Provide general upper body strengthening exercises, including wheelbarrow walking, animal walks, chin-ups, swinging on monkey bars, tug of war, pushing or pulling weighted objects.

- Practice fine motor activities at a vertical work surface, such as a table easel, chalkboard, or piece of large paper taped to the wall. When the hand works at eye level in this position, the wrist is automatically extended, which helps to develop the needed stability. Also, using the arm against the pull of gravity helps to strengthen shoulder muscles. If the child is not able to hold a crayon or marker with the fingers in this position, you may provide tiny bits of broken crayon or chalk as an alternative, as this will also help to strengthen the fingers. Nonwriting activities, such as building a collage, using ink stamps, or placing stickers on a vertical work surface, are other good alternatives.

- Encourage plenty of floor time, where the child lies on his or her tummy while reading, watching television, or playing games. This position requires the child to bear his or her upper body weight on the elbows or forearms, which helps to develop strength in these joints.

- Teach the child to perform "sitting push-ups" by placing his or her hands along the side of the chair, and pushing up on the arms so that the buttocks are lifted slightly off of the chair.

To develop finger isolation and dexterity

- Cup the palm of the hand, and try to fill it with rice or sand. The more the hand can hold, the better developed are the arches of the hand.

- Store favorite toys in plastic storage bags with a zipper or pinch-type closure. When the child puts his or her toys away, there will be a natural opportunity to develop pinch strength.

- Use spring-type clothes fasteners to attach pictures to a clothes line or to the edges of a cardboard box.

- For the child who has a mature pencil grasp, practice coloring in tiny, miniature pictures as this requires using very small, controlled movements of the marker or crayon.

- Use tweezers, strawberry hullers, tongs, or other pinch-type tools to sort small objects into different containers. This can be timed to make a race.

- Roll out tiny balls of clay, papier mâché, or tissue paper using the tips of the finger, and use these to glue onto paper to make a collage.

- Practice finger pattern games, such as learning sign language, making finger shadows, or playing with finger puppets.

- Practice shuffling and holding a set of cards.

- Hold a large coin with the tips of the thumb and fingers around the edge of the coin, and try to rotate the coin 360 degrees.

- Hold a cardboard or plastic bowl with one hand, palm facing up towards the ceiling, and attempt to rotate the bowl using only the fingers of that hand. Fill the bowl with water, rice, or sand for added difficulty.

- Play tug of war with a coin to encourage pinch strength.

- Using one hand at a time, practice squirreling small objects into and out of the palm one at a time (i.e. pick up the first object with the thumb and forefinger and transfer it to the palm of the hand, then hold it there while picking up a second, then third, then fourth item). See how many items the child can get before dropping one.

- Use hole punches or craft punches to make tiny shapes to use as "confetti" or to glue onto art projects.

Functional vision skills

As was discussed in Chapter 1, children with coordination difficulties often have associated problems with functional vision skills. Different than problems affecting eyesight (such as blindness or nearsightedness), functional vision refers to the way the various eye muscles move efficiently to track a moving target. Children with problems affecting bilateral motor integration are particularly susceptible to difficulties with tracking a visual target across their midline, or to accommodating vision to focus on objects at varying distances from the eyes. One way to screen for these problems is to hold a small toy approximately 12 inches from the child, and ask the child to follow the toy with the eyes (not moving the head) as you move it horizontally, vertically or diagonally. Look for problems including a sudden blink or jerk in the eyes as the target reaches midline. Children with problems visually crossing the midline may also show signs of fatigue when reading or performing other visual work. They may rub their eyes or complain of discomfort, lose their place easily, or avoid such tasks altogether. If problems in this area are suspected, parents should seek the advice of an eye specialist. Nurses and occupational therapists are often capable of screening for these problems. Most eye doctors are prepared to evaluate only serious problems affecting functional vision. A developmental-behavioral optometrist has the specialized training and experience to provide in-depth evaluation of more subtle functional vision problems.

If problems are identified, the professionals involved can suggest strategies that are specific to the child's particular weaknesses. The following suggestions are helpful for most children.

Suggested activities for preventing eyestrain

- During reading and writing, take frequent visual "breaks" by looking up and focusing on a distant target for about ten seconds.

- Try to use incandescent or natural light for work areas whenever possible, as fluorescent light is much harsher. For close visual activities, light on the work surface should be about three times brighter than the surrounding light.

- Avoid glare on work surfaces. Never place a computer or television screen directly in front of a window unless there are drapes or curtains available to block the light. Placing a blotter or large piece of dark construction paper on a desk can reduce glare from fluorescent lights.

- Try to read or do other close visual work at an eye-to-activity distance that is approximately equal to the distance between the elbow and the middle knuckles.

- Consider using a bookrest to help the child to maintain an upright posture when reading. This creates less stress on the eyes than reading a book placed flat on the desk, because all of the lines of print are at an equal distance from the eyes.

- Television should be viewed from a distance of eight to ten feet from the screen, and while sitting upright. Take care to avoid glare on the screen from lamps or windows.

To strengthen functional vision

- Suspend a lightweight plastic ball on a string from the ceiling. Give the child a dowel that is marked with different bands of color on the left side (blue), right side (red), and middle (yellow). Ask the child to start by tapping the ball smoothly and rhythmically using the middle (yellow) part of the dowel. Gradually increase the difficulty by having the child tap out "patterns" such as red-blue-red-blue, etc. This requires considerable eye–hand coordination and bilateral skill.

- Sit in a dark room and use a flashlight to draw large shapes or letters on a distant wall, while the child guesses what has been drawn.

- Play flashlight "tag" in a dark room. The adult moves his or her flashlight in a random pattern on the wall while the child tries to follow with another flashlight.

- Have the child hold one paddle in each hand, then try to bat a balloon back and forth as many times as possible without dropping the balloon.

- Take a page from a magazine (size of print depending on the child's age) and have him or her trace the lines with a pencil from left to right while looking for specified items (e.g. cross out all the "t"s or draw a circle around all the words beginning with the letter "b").

- Mazes, dot to dots, and labyrinth games are all helpful for developing visual tracking skillst — he larger the better, because size will help assure that the child uses his or her eyes across the midline.

- Cut the bottoms off of two large plastic milk bottles or detergent bottles. Use these to play "scoop catch" with a beanbag or koosh ball. Ask the child to hold one bottle in each hand and practice tossing the beanbag from hand to hand for added bilateral control.

Oral-motor skills

As was discussed in Chapter 1, problems with oral-motor skills may be present in children with other types of coordination difficulties. Problems in this area can impact upon speech and eating skills, and will usually require intervention from a specialist. The following are some simple activities that can help to build strength and coordination in the muscles that support speech and oral control.

- Practice making faces and imitating facial movements in front of a mirror.

- Use a lollipop or other edible prop and play "catch the lollipop," having the child chase the moving target with his or her tongue.

- Use whistles, bubble wands, and other toys that involve blowing to strengthen lip closure.

- Practice using a straw to blow a feather, ping pong ball or other lightweight target across the room.

- Suck into a straw to pick up a small piece of tissue paper that is then transferred to a container.

- Use a straw to suck up thickened food, such as pureed fruit, yogurt, or soft ice cream.

- Place a piece of cereal, raisin, or small candy piece on the child's tongue, and have the child move it to different locations in the mouth using only the tongue.

- Place individual alphabet cereal pieces on the child's tongue and have the child guess what letter it is.

Chapter 5

TEACHING INDEPENDENCE IN DAILY LIVING SKILLS

One of the most basic aspects of growing up is learning to become independent in the activities of self care: eating, dressing, using the toilet, bathing, washing one's hair, preparing a snack, making a bed, and all the other many and varied tasks of daily living. Children with coordination difficulties may be delayed in achieving self-care independence for a variety of reasons. First, problems with coordination may interfere with the completion of the task itself. It is difficult, for example, to learn to button if the fingers are not strong enough to maintain a pinch on the button while maneuvering it through the buttonhole. Bending over to pull up pants or to put on socks may be difficult if balance is challenged. Or, difficulties with motor planning and bilateral integration may make learning the steps involved in tying shoes a daunting undertaking. Second, factors related to the home and family environment can impact upon the child's learning. Children with coordination difficulties are almost always slower than average in completing self-care tasks. They also may show less skill in completing tasks than same-age peers. For example, the child may be able to get his or her clothes on correctly, but leave shirts untucked and buttons misaligned. Or, they may use the toilet independently but have difficulty wiping themselves thoroughly or washing their hands effectively. It is not uncommon for parents to feel embarrassed by their child's unkempt appearance, or frustrated by their slow pace when schedules are pressing, and to take over those activities that the child should really be expected to complete on his or her own. This can lead to a pattern of over-dependence in the child, and may cause parents to feel frustrated and resentful. The following general suggestions may be helpful in teaching self-care independence in the child:

- Remember that self-care skills may develop slower than in typical development, and be patient as the child acquires new skills. Table 1.1

reviewed typical milestones of personal-social development, and this may be used as a basis for anticipating developmental sequences in self care. Understanding that the child may have difficulty with motor planning, choose no more than one or two skills to work on at a time.

- Children have variable levels of motivation to develop self-care independence. When possible, select goals that are driven by the child's interests and motivation. Always remember that children are most motivated when provided with positive behavior supports, so try to "catch" the child trying to doing something independently, and be sure to reward the effort. If either you or the child are becoming too frustrated, it is best to shift focus to a new goal that might allow the child to experience success.

- Practicing self-care skills requires an investment of time on the part of both the child and the adult who is helping. Try to identify times during the day that are less stressful for practice of essential skills. For example, there may be more stress in the morning when getting dressed for school than when changing clothes after school to go out to play.

- Whenever possible, reduce the complexity or number of steps involved in learning a new task. For example, washing hair with shampoo with built-in conditioner is easier than washing in two steps, and putting on a two-piece exercise suit is less complicated than an outfit with many layers and fasteners.

- Many children benefit from picture charts to help them remember essential steps in completing self-care tasks.

- The backward chaining technique, described in Chapter 3, may be a useful strategy for learning new skills.

Suggested strategies for dressing skills

- Provide a picture chart to show the child the order in which to don clothes.

- Children with balance difficulties or poor postural stability may benefit from sitting on the floor or on a low step stool with their back resting against a wall or other supporting surface.

- Allow the child to have reasonable choices in clothing selection, even if the child's taste differs from your own, as this may help with motivation.

- Most children learn best when their wardrobe is limited to a few items of each type. For example, zippers differ slightly from jacket to jacket, and it is easiest to learn one zipper on one jacket at a time.

- Loose fitting or slightly oversized clothing is easiest to learn to manage independently.

- Create a "dress up" box of special clothing purchased from thrift shops to allow the child to practice dressing skills during leisure time. Other opportunities for practicing dressing skills exist in dolls with clothes, backpacks, etc.

- Larger buttons are easiest to learn. Try removing buttons, then re-sewing them more loosely and wrapping the thread several times around the base to give the child more freedom of movement when manipulating the button. If the child has severe difficulty learning to button, velcro closures may be sewn on instead.

- For the child who confuses right and left, or front and back, use clothing markers to "code" the orientation of clothes. For example, a red dot placed inside a shoe indicates the right foot, and a blue dot inside the collar of a sweater means it marks the back of the sweater.

- Shoe tying can be particularly challenging, and is best learned using backwards chaining. Try buying two pairs of laces in different colors, cutting each set in half and then re-tying them so each lace has a different color on each side. This can help the child to visualize the various steps. If shoe tying is too challenging, using velcro closures, curly elastic shoelaces, slip-ons or jungle slides can be reasonable alternatives, but make sure the shoes stay on the child's feet tightly enough to provide the proper support.

- Tube socks are usually easier to don than those that have a well-defined heel.

- Remember that children with sensory modulation difficulties may be particularly sensitive to the "feel" of certain clothing. Often, children with this problem like to have their arms and legs covered even in hot weather, dislike scratchy clothing tags or tight elastic closures, and prefer soft, conforming fabrics like sweats or fleece. You may wish to purchase a stitch-remover which can be used to remove annoying labels from collars.

Suggested strategies for mealtimes

- For some children, sensory defensiveness causes them to have extreme aversion to certain food tastes or textures, which can lead to overly picky eating, parent–child distress during mealtimes, and, in some extreme cases, malnutrition. Professional advice from an occupational therapist with experience can help to design a program of oral desensitization and to gradually advance acceptance of a wider variety of foods.

- Keep portions small when introducing new foods, and praise the child for attempting even a tiny "taste."

- Allow the child to help in determining the menu and preparing food, even if his or her choice is not the most "nutritionally correct," to reinforce participation in the mealtime.

- Be tolerant and patient of accidental spills, but expect the child to assume responsibility for at least a portion of the clean-up after the meal is completed.

- Be sure that the seating arrangement provides good support in sitting and is at a height that allows elbows to rest comfortably on the table and feet to lie flat on the floor.

- Non-slip placemats help to stabilize plates and bowls when learning to use utensils.

- Deeper plates and bowls are easier to learn to scoop from than a shallow plate. When first learning to scoop with a spoon, thicker foods such as pudding will be easier to scoop than thinner foods such as pureed fruit.

- Use two-handled cups, "sippy" cups, or cups with a built-in straw to develop control.

Suggested strategies for personal hygiene

- When developing toileting skills, be sure the child wears clothes that are easy to pull on and off, such as loosely fitting elastic pants. This will help to prevent "accidents" that may occur if the child struggles to arrange his or her clothes for toileting.

- Some children with low muscle tone have lower than average awareness that they need to void, and benefit from frequent prompts or reminders to try to use the toilet.

- Look for commercially available toilet paper that has visual reminders for the child to know how much paper is the "right" amount.

- Have wet wipes close at hand to help assure thorough cleaning after a bowel movement.

- Arrange the bathroom so that all necessary materials are within easy reach of the child, and that there are few distractions to prevent the child from focusing on the task at hand.

- For the child with sensory defensiveness, use firm strokes when washing or drying with a towel. Some children prefer to be wrapped in a terry cloth robe instead of being rubbed dry with a towel.

- Electric toothbrushes are easier for some children. In addition, the vibration often helps the child with oral sensitivity to tolerate the brushing more comfortably. Vary the temperature of the water and the flavor of the toothpaste according to the child's preferences.

- Toothpaste may be easier to dispense from a pump than from a squeeze tube.

- Hair-washing is particularly stressful for some children. The position of sitting with the head tipped back to avoid getting soap in the eyes is challenging to the child's postural control, and can be frightening for the child who needs the visual input of having his or her head in vertical alignment with space. Try mounting a mirror so the child can see his or her head position, or use nonirritating baby shampoo and let the child wash hair with his or her head tipped forward.

Chapter 6

ADDRESSING PROBLEMS WITH CLASSROOM SKILLS

Once the child reaches the age of entering school, great importance is placed on learning to manage the tools of the classroom, such as pencil, sharpener, crayon, scissors, glue bottle, and other manipulatives. Early childhood educators universally recognize the importance of "hands-on" learning approaches to the developing mind. As a result, young children spend large portions of their school day engaged in activities that not only ask them to think and learn, but that also challenge their motor skills in a variety of ways. The child with coordination difficulties can quickly become discouraged if found lacking in these skills. Parents and teachers are sometimes reluctant to seek help for the child in the belief that the problem is developmental in nature and will become less problematic over time. While this may be true for some children, others find it impossible to "catch up" and must cope with falling farther and farther behind in schoolwork. The following sections will discuss some of the strategies that may be considered by teachers and parents to help the student cope with demands in the classroom.

Seating and positioning

The importance of proper seating at school, and at home when doing homework, cannot be overemphasized. A large percentage of children with developmental coordination disorders have problems with posture as a result of low muscle tone. This can impact the child's ability to have a stable base upon which to produce controlled arm and hand movement, and can also have an effect on the child's attention and visual control. Children with poor postural control often find it extremely tiring to have to sit upright for long periods of time, and find comfort in fidgeting, slouching, or leaning on the table, all of which interfere with their attention and motor control. Young children should not be asked to sit still for more than 15 minutes at a time, and benefit from frequent opportunities to stretch or to have a motor "break." Children should be encouraged to sit with their hips well back in the chair, and the chair should be of such a size as to allow sitting with hips, knees, and ankles all at 90° angles (see Figure 6.1).

Figure 6.1 Proper height of desk and chair

Chairs with flat seats are better than those with rounded seats for most children. The rounded seat encourages the hips to tilt backwards, a position that makes it hard to sit upright. It is important for chair legs to be of equal length, as uneven legs encourage rocking and tipping in the chair. The table height should be two inches above the elbow when in a seated position. Desks that are too high cause the child to elevate the shoulders when working, a position that limits smooth controlled movement at the shoulder. Desks that are too low contribute to slouching. Most children demonstrate better posture when seated at a square or rectangular table than when seated at a round table, because rounded tables provide less surface for stabilizing the elbows during seatwork. The depth of the desk should be sufficient for the paper to be at least six inches away from the edge to allow sufficient room for resting the arms on the desk. Children with very low tone may benefit from a table with a semicircle cutout. This allows the child to pull up to the cutout and have maximal support for the arms. Teachers should keep in mind that children come in all shapes and sizes, and so should classroom seating arrangements! Uniform desk and seat size will almost always be detrimental to at least some students.

Care should also be given to the arrangement of desks in the classroom. Ideally, all students should be facing in the same direction when observing the teacher demonstrating something that involves motor learning, such as letter strokes or the instructions for a fine motor craft. Students who observe a teacher's movements face-on are receiving a different mental "picture" of the instruction to those who are looking at the teacher's side. Students who have yet to determine a hand preference or who have significant difficulties with bilateral motor integration and crossing the midline should be seated centrally, because turning the head to look at the teacher can influence which hand will be chosen. In general, left-handed students should sit on the left side of the room, facing the teacher, and right-handed students should be on the right. The slight head turning needed to look at the teacher triggers reflexive body movements that are more comfortable for students so positioned.

It is also important to consider lighting in the workspace. Avoid lighting arrangements that may cause glare or that will project a shadow onto the student's work, as this will make it more difficult to concentrate on the work.

The following are seating and positioning accommodations that may be worth consideration:

- Use dycem or other nonslip mats on the seat surface to decrease squirming.

- Students who have very poor upper body posture when seated at a desk may benefit from having a two to three inch wedge placed on their chair so the wide end of the wedge is toward the front of the seat. This places the hips in a position of slight flexion, which helps some children to maintain postural tone.

- Other strategies to provide body awareness needed to maintain erect posture might include: frequent opportunities to get up and move around or stretch; periodically putting downward pressure on the student's shoulders; teaching the child to do "chair sit-ups" where hands are placed on the side of the chair, and with downward pressure the child lifts his or her bottom one inch off the chair surface.

- Placing rubber crutch tips or tennis balls with cuts in the surface on chair legs helps some students to keep their chair in position.

- During circle time, children with poor upright posture should be allowed to sit with their back supported against a piece of furniture.

- Many students benefit from working at an elevated writing surface, angled to at least 30°. This helps to support posture, and places the wrist in a comfortable position for writing. Furthermore, it encourages the student to keep his or her head more upright during work, which can help to improve attention. Slant boards are commercially available, and come with a variety of special features such as clamps to hold paper. Alternatively, use a sturdy three-ring binder placed on its side.

- For students with visual inattentiveness, consider seating placement that minimizes distractions. The student's desk should not face a cluttered bulletin board or a window overlooking the playground. The student may attend best if seated at the front of the class, so other students are behind him or her, and should be paired with students who sit and work quietly. If necessary, a study carrel can provide a quiet place to attend to classwork.

Remember that correct seating and positioning is important at the computer station as well. Ideally, shared computer work spaces should be fully adjustable to fit the needs of different-sized users. Monitors should be placed at the student's eye level, about an arm's length away from the student, and away from sources of glare such as overhead lights or a window. The computer station chair should fit the student as described in the above section. The keyboard should be at a negative angle, or can be placed on a pillow in the student's lap. Wrist guards are helpful for some students who need support for keeping the wrists in a neutral position. Sitting at a computer for long periods of time can be tiring, especially for children who have difficulty maintaining erect posture. For this reason, rest and stretch breaks should be enforced at approximately 15-minute intervals.

Learning to write

Learning to write is a challenge for most students, including those with typical motor development. It is nevertheless a critically important skill to master, as learning to write fluently can be a tool for remembering and processing information as well as communicating thoughts and ideas. For students with developmental motor concerns, writing may be one of the biggest problems faced in school.

Writing is a complex motor act that requires a number of prerequisite skills, including good postural control, the ability to make isolated movements of the small muscles in the hand, eye–hand coordination, establishment of a dominant hand, motor planning, visual discrimination, perceptual organization, and cognitive/language processing. For many children, writing is taught before these prerequisite skills have fully developed, and instruction then proceeds at a very rapid pace throughout the early school years. Given large class sizes, teachers must provide group instruction in penmanship. Although most teachers are keen observers of their students' legibility, they may fail to notice when individual students develop poor habits such as making letter strokes in the wrong direction, or using poor posture or hand grasp during writing. Even when the observant teacher notices such problems, he or she has limited time to intervene with the small number of students who are struggling with this aspect of their learning. This is especially true when the student is intelligent, and is able to demonstrate his or her knowledge through verbal interactions. Unfortunately, poor handwriting habits can become firmly embedded in the child's pattern of writing and, once learned, can be very difficult to change. It is important for parents and teachers to attend to handwriting difficulties as soon as they are observed, and to try to intervene before bad habits develop. Parents and teachers should also recognize that there will be natural variations in handwriting skill, and that some allowances should be made for individual differences. One only needs to look at the handwriting of adults to appreciate this! Students who display stylistic differences involving letter size, slant, or unique formations may be perfectly capable of getting the written word down on paper—they just do it their own way. Table 6.1 describes characteristics of handwriting that may be considered dysfunctional and in need of professional help.

Table 6.1 Characteristics of dysfunctional handwriting

- Writing is illegible, despite good effort and attention to writing
- Student forgets how to form letters, or uses an inconsistent approach to forming letters
- Problems with spatial organization lead to many reversals (normal through first grade), or severely impaired spacing
- Writing speed is slow and prevents completion of assignments within the allotted time
- Writing causes hand-fatigue leading to avoidance and incomplete assignments
- Writing process requires so much effort that the student is unable to concentrate on the content of his or her writing
- Expressive language is much less developed in writing than in oral expression

Several assessment tools are available for more formal assessment of handwriting skill. Some may be given to a class as a group, while others are designed for individual administration. Because of the variability in instructional strategies and student differences, it is hard to compare a student's performance to a normative group meaningfully. However, use of formal handwriting assessment can often be helpful in delineating a student's particular weaknesses, setting appropriate goals, and measuring progress. Examples of commercially available handwriting assessment tools can be found in Appendix I.

Suggestions for strategies to help with various aspects of handwriting difficulty are discussed on the next page.

Holding the pencil correctly

The optimal way to hold a pencil is using a dynamic tripod grasp, illustrated in Figure 6.2. In this position, the wrist is extended (bent back) slightly, which helps to position the fingers in opposition around the pencil shaft. The thumb is flexed (bent toward the palm) and touches the pencil with the flat surface of the pad. The area of the hand that lies between the index finger and the thumb, known as the thumb web space, is open and rounded. This position allows the wrist to be the dominant force in forming horizontal strokes, and the fingers to be the dominant force in forming vertical or rounded strokes. Children who hold their pencil in this position can work longer and with less hand-fatigue than children who use other types of grasp.

Figure 6.2 Dynamic tripod grasp

Children who adopt other pencil grasps do so for a variety of reasons. In some cases, it is simply due to the fact that no one ever taught the child the correct position. Other children have low muscle tone, and lack the strength and stability to use the dynamic tripod grasp. They may attempt to hold the pencil in different ways that provide them with a comfortable degree of stability, but limit their ability to make small, isolated movements of the fingers needed for writing. Commonly, children with low tone have instability at the base of the thumb, and hold their pencil using a lateral tripod grasp with the thumb wrapped around the shaft and/or the index finger, as illustrated in Figure 6.3.

Figure 6.3 Lateral tripod grasp

This position is not necessarily dysfunctional, as long as the child can make small finger movements during writing and does not complain of fatigue or hand pain. Some children with instability at the thumb and index finger can be taught to use the modified tripod grasp, illustrated in Figure 6.4, as an alternative.

Figure 6.4 Modified tripod grasp

Changing a child's pencil grasp works best for young children who have not yet formed a specific pattern, and who periodically change positions on their own. It may also be successful for motivated students who have concern about the quality of their handwriting. Once a pencil grasp is firmly established, whether right or wrong, it is very difficult to change. Suggestions for coping with an immature pencil grasp include the following:

- A variety of commercially available pencil grips are available. Some serve to position the fingers in the correct tripod position. Others are designed to help with excessively tight grasp. Most children can immediately identify whether a particular grip is helpful to them. Children are often motivated by selecting the color or style of a grip, but those who reject a grip should not be forced to use one. Place a colored dot or small sticker on the spot where the thumb should go to help the child remember the correct finger placement.

- Homemade "grips" can be fabricated by wrapping a rubber band around the shaft, or by molding cotton or foam around the shaft and holding it in place with fabric tape to make a cushioned grip.

- Provide opportunities for the student to write or perform other fine motor activities at a vertical work surface, such as an easel or chalkboard, to help develop wrist strength and stability (see Figure 6.5). Lying on the floor and writing on a clipboard is another way to help build wrist strength and stability.

- For children who grasp the pencil tightly within the thumb web space, try putting the pencil through a large bead or styrofoam ball to make a

Figure 6.5 Writing at a vertical surface

large rounded grasp, use large-diameter writing tools, or try using tiny tools such as golf pencils or broken pieces of crayon.

- For students with shaky movements or tremors, try using a heavy, weighted pencil. These are commercially available, or can be handmade by putting the pencil through a series of metal bolts or washers and gluing in place at the top of the pencil.

- For students who press down too hard on the paper, place a piece of cardboard under the paper and demonstrate that if the point of the pencil pokes through to the cardboard, he or she is pressing too hard. Provide opportunities to practice writing on tissue paper or paper towels that will rip given excessive pressure. Or, try using mechanical pencils, as the thin lead points will break if excessive pressure is used.

- For students who seem to have weak pressure, try to increase the resistance to writing. Place paper over a piece of sandpaper or other textured surface. Or, place worksheets inside a plastic sheet protector and use a grease marker to write on the surface. Use of a soft lead pencil can also help to increase the visibility of their writing.

- Encourage practice by offering many choices of writing tool, such as markers, gel pens, vibrating pens.

- Assure that the paper is aligned properly by placing a strip of masking tape on the writing surface to mark the correct angle of the paper (see Figure 6.6). For right-handed students, this would be approximately 20° to 30° toward the left. Most left-handed students prefer a slightly greater slant of 30° to 35° to the right. If the student has an individual desk, you can also cut a triangle to tape in the corner of the desk. The student is taught to hold the paper so the top is parallel to the bottom of the triangle as a visual guide.

Figure 6.6 Use of masking tape to mark the correct slant for right-and left-handed writers

Making letters correctly

Many students struggle with learning how to form letters using the correct strokes. This is not surprising, considering that kindergarten students who have just mastered learning to draw a cross and square must, within their first school year, learn 26 uppercase and lowercase letters and commit them all to memory! In this age of technology, some schools place less emphasis on learning the basic mechanics of handwriting, knowing that most students will eventually complete the majority of their written assignments on a word processor. Computers cannot, however, replace the need to write class notes, fill out a job application, sign checks, and complete a wide array of other tasks that involve using a pencil or pen. It is essential that schools adopt a specific handwriting curriculum to teach, and that teachers are encouraged to adhere to the curriculum and to offer students multiple opportunities for practice. Selection of a handwriting curriculum is not easy given the many programs that are available. For example, some programs emphasize a straight up-and-down manuscript style while others favor a slanted or italicized manuscript style in the belief that this will help the student to make an easier transition to cursive. Table 6.2 provides examples of popular handwriting programs.

Once a writing style has been selected, the student needs frequent opportunities to practice the correct letter stroke formations. Parents or classroom volunteers can be engaged in helping with this task, since there is often not sufficient classroom time to allow repeated practice. As letters are first taught, the supervising adult needs to observe for incorrect stroke formations, and intervene before bad habits have had the chance to develop. Parents should be encouraged to build opportunities for practicing writing into motivating activities during the day. Writing a pen-pal letter, copying the family's grocery list and adding a favorite treat, or writing a schedule of television shows to be watched during the week are more motivating forms of practice than simply doing worksheets. The following are suggestions for helping children learn correct letter stroke formations:

- Before teaching specific letters, it is important to ensure that the child understands the concepts such as up, down, across, over, under, slide up or down (diagonal), and can copy these strokes upon a verbal request.

- Initial teaching should be performed in a vertical plane, since the concepts "up" and "down" mean something different when performed at a desk. Teachers should make sure that when teaching a letter for the first time, all children are directly facing his or her model. The teacher should face away from the students, and draw the letter in the air or on the board while slowly articulating the sequence of strokes.

- Rather than teaching letters in the logical sequence of the alphabet, consider grouping letters according to similarities in stroke formation. For example, lowercase manuscript letters a, g, and q all begin with a slightly elongated circle that is formed in a counterclockwise direction. Lowercase h, l, k, and t all begin with a down stroke that starts on the upper guide line. Teaching these letters as a group can help the student with motor memory for correct stroke direction, because they are rehearsing the same motion for these letters.

- Following dotted line paths to form letters can be helpful, as long as the student is following the direction of the strokes correctly.

- Tracing sandpaper or other textured letters helps some students develop kinesthetic memory for the strokes. Make sure that the student is tracing in the correct direction.

- To help with motor memory for letters, try having students guess a letter drawn with your finger on their back, or have them trace letters in the air with their eyes closed.

- Writing against resistance can help with kinesthetic memory for letter strokes. Try placing sandpaper or soft construction paper under the writing paper, or use a soft lead pencil or grease marker.

- Letter reversals are common through first grade. If the child has significant difficulty with reversals, start by assessing whether it is a visual perception problem or a motor learning problem. The student who cannot match letters visually needs practice with this before the letter formation is taught. Students who can recognize letters correctly but draw them reversed benefit from strategies to increase kinesthetic awareness of letter strokes.

- Be sure to provide an alphabet strip for reference on the student's desk. If the student is confused about the correct direction of letter strokes, it may help to draw a tiny green dot for "go" at the starting point for each letter.

- Instruct students to grade their own work according to specified standards as a method to increase self awareness. Ask the student to circle his or her best letter, and to draw a line under the one that needs more practice.

Table 6.2 Handwriting programs

Big Strokes for Little Folks (manuscript) by Bonnie Levine Rubell	Harcourt Assessment Inc. 19500 Bulverde Road San Antonio, TX 78259-3701 Tel: (800) 211-8378 www.harcourtassessment.com
D'Nealian Handwriting Program (slanted manuscript and cursive) by Donald Neal Thurber	Modern Curriculum Press Pearson Learning Group 135 South Mount Zion Road P.O. Box 2500 Lebanon, IN 46052 Tel: (800) 526-9907 www.pearsonlearning.com
Handwriting Without Tears (prewriting, manuscript and cursive) by Janice Z. Olsen	8001 MacArthur Boulevard Cabin John, MD 20818 Tel: (301) 263-2700 www.hwtears.com
Italic handwriting (slanted manuscript and cursive) by Barbara Getty and Inga Dubay Portland State University, Extended Studies	Continuing Education Press P.O. Box 1394 Portland, OR 97207-1394 Tel: (503) 725-4891 www.cep.pdx.edu
Loops and Other Groups (cursive) by Mary D. Benbow	Harcourt Assessment Inc. 19500 Bulverde San Antonio, TX 78259-3701 Tel: (800) 211-8378 www.harcourtassessment.com
The Sensible Hand (manuscript and cursive) by L.C. Becht	American Occupational Therapy Association 4720 Montgomery Lane P.O. Box 31220 Bethesda, MD 20824-1220 Tel: (301) 652-2682 www.aota.org
Zaner-Bloser Handwriting (manuscript and cursive)	Zaner-Bloser Educational Publishers 2200 West Fifth Avenue P.O. Box 16764 Columbus, OH 43216-6764 Tel: (800) 421-3018 www.zaner-bloser.com

Spacing and staying on the line

Difficulties with line placement and spacing are common and can significantly impact the legibility of writing. Many students, when first learning to write, forget to leave spaces or to think about where to place the letter on the line because they are concentrating so hard on just getting the letter formation correct that they cannot concentrate on anything else. Although these aspects of penmanship should be taught from the start, it is probably best to have conservative expectations of the student's performance until letter formations are automatic. Traditionally, students are initially taught to write using wide-ruled paper in the belief that they lack the fine motor control needed to make smaller letters. In reality, some young children actually do better given narrow-ruled paper. To find what is comfortable for students, ask them to write their name or to copy a sentence on a piece of blank paper using their very best writing. Measure the height of the letters to determine the most comfortable fit for rule. The following suggestions may be helpful for teaching a student the correct line placement and spacing for writing:

- Experiment with different types of paper that color code the guide lines. Many students benefit from having different color guide lines, but for some students, it presents too much visual information and is confusing to them. Some students do best with single-rule paper. Others benefit from having a yellow highlight marker drawn through the lower half of the line.

- Paper with slightly raised lines is commercially available and can offer a tactual cue for starting and stopping strokes. A homemade version can be made by using a dressmaker's tracing wheel and, with a ruler, tracing the guide lines from the back of the paper.

- Use a piece of clear tape run down the right and left sides of the paper to remind the student to leave margins. Highlighting or placing tape on alternate rows of lined paper can help to remind the student to skip lines between sentences.

- For students who have trouble writing from left to right across the page, draw a green line to mark the left-hand margin, and a red line to mark the right-hand margin. This cues the student where to start and stop on the line.

- Teach students to leave a finger space between words. If this is confusing, or if their fingers get in the way, teach them to leave a dash between each word, then phase out the dashes when spacing is relatively consistent.

- Teach the student to check his or her work for spacing using a finger or a strip of paper to check between each word. Provide rewards for students who leave appropriate spaces, for example, placing a piece of cereal or other tiny treat on each appropriate space.

- Consider practicing writing on graph paper for some assignments, and teach the student to leave a blank box between each word. Graph paper also works well for students who have difficulty aligning number columns during math assignments.

Special considerations for left-handed students

Approximately 10 percent of students are naturally left handed. These students face some additional challenges in learning to write, especially if they have coordination difficulties. Left-handed students are at a disadvantage when learning to write, because as they work across the page in a left-to-right direction, their hand covers up what they have just written, reducing the visual feedback from their product. As a result, many left-handed students adopt an awkward pencil grasp where the wrist is bent forward into a "hooked" position. This allows them to see what they are writing, but is a very inefficient grasp that can be fatiguing during longer periods of writing. Use of a vertical or slanted writing surface can help to decrease the tendency to "hook." It is also important to teach the student to angle the paper correctly (about 30° towards the right, or aligned parallel to the writing arm—see Figure 6.6). Other suggestions for helping left-handed writers are as follows:

- Teach the student to hold the pencil about one inch away from the lead. This will allow a small space for viewing the letters as they are drawn. Use a small piece of colored tape, a rubber band, or a foam grip to mark the correct location to place fingers.

- Encourage learning to write with a slight slant towards the left, opposite to that which is expected of right-handed students. Prepare alphabet strips that demonstrate the appropriate slant.

- If the student is having difficulty learning correct letter formations, use your left hand to demonstrate the correct stroke formations.

- Seat left-handed students at the midline or on the left side of material to be copied from the board.

- Left-handed students have difficulty writing on binders or workbooks that have the rings on the left side of the page, as these interfere with their writing arm. Either purchase top-bound books, or orient books so that the student writes on an inverted page, with the rings towards the right.

- Many worksheets have a word or sentence to be copied with a blank space to the right of the word. This is difficult for the left-handed student, as the writing arm will cover the model during writing. Consider preparing different models for right- and left-handed students, or having material organized so that blank spaces are placed underneath the model.

- Group students according to right- or left-handedness. This will help to discourage elbow bumping, and also allows the teacher to provide accommodations as a group.

Accommodations for older students with handwriting problems

For some students with significant motor learning difficulties, handwriting problems persist and become increasingly problematic as the demands for high volumes of writing increase. For these students, it is often necessary to provide significant accommodations to allow them to demonstrate their acquisition of knowledge without the great demands on writing. The following are suggestions for appropriate writing accommodations:

- Word-processing skills, including keyboarding, should be taught at an early age. Although typing cannot fully replace the need for handwriting, it can provide a significantly more efficient means of producing written assignments.

- Allow the student additional time to complete written assignments.

- Allow the student to give taped or oral reports instead of a written report.

- For lengthy assignments that must be copied from the board, provide a photocopy of the teacher's notes.

- Allow tape recording to replace lecture notes, or provide a photocopy of a fellow student's handwritten notes.

- Allow the student to dictate a report to a parent or friend who writes the report, quoting the student verbatim.

- Allow the student to take oral exams to replace or supplement written exams.

- Reduce the volume of copying necessary. For example, provide an outline of the lecture with headings so the student must only record the details, or provide math worksheets that already have the problems written instead of having the student copy problems from the board.

- Provide a writing binder that includes samples of correct letter formations and templates of common worksheets for the student to refer to.

- Be aware that some students write illegibly to hide the fact that they have trouble spelling. Provide spelling and vocabulary reference lists as needed.

- If a student has many issues affecting handwriting, do not overwhelm him or her by correcting every error. Focus on one problem at a time, such as staying on the line, or putting a space between words.

- Allow the student to use the tools, paper, and style of writing that is most comfortable. Reduce the expectations for neatness and spelling, at least for first drafts of work.

- Encourage the student to learn to use abbreviations to reduce work in note-taking.

Scissor skills

Using scissors is a complicated motor skill that is hard for many young children to learn. The appropriate way to hold scissors, with the thumb in the small loop and facing upwards, the middle and ring finger through the larger loop, the index finger curled over the larger loop to provide stability, and the ring and pinky finger curled into the palm for strength, is illustrated in Figure 6.7.

Figure 6.7 Correct scissors grasp

This skill does not develop until at least four years of age, and much later in children with developmental motor concerns. A common grasp used by children with low muscle tone, illustrated in Figure 6.8, is the *pronated scissors grasp*, which leaves the thumb pointing down towards the table and the other fingers extended.

Figure 6.8 Pronated scissors grasp

This position is very inefficient and should be discouraged. Table 6.3 explains some of the prerequisite motor skills that must be in place for the child to learn scissoring in an effective manner.

Table 6.3 Prerequisites for learning to use scissors

- Ability to pay attention
- Ability to open/close hand without spreading the fingers
- Ability for one hand to move in a different way to the other hand (holding/cutting)
- Ability to use the eyes to follow the hand in motion (eye–hand coordination)
- Adequate tone/strength to stabilize the shoulder, elbow, forearm and wrist during cutting
- Adequate sensory feedback to calibrate motion (right amount of force and propulsion)

Research shows that girls tend to develop scissor skills slightly earlier than boys, but that for either gender, skill is not mature until first grade. Scissoring is typically introduced in the preschool years, and receives a variable amount of practice depending upon the individual child's situation. Table 6.4 presents the developmental progression of scissor skills in children with typical motor development.

The following suggestions may be helpful for the child who is having difficulty learning how to use scissors.

Difficulty opening and closing the scissors

- Practice games that involve squeezing and letting go (use a turkey baster to fill a cup with water, or tongs to pick up objects to fill a container).

- Practice games that require pinching with the thumb (punching out shapes with a craft punch, squeezing a clothes pin, etc.).

Table 6.4 Developmental expectations for scissoring

30 months	Knows where to place fingers and can snip but not cut
36 months	Follows line to cut a 6 inch piece of paper into two pieces
	Static bilateral control (hands stay in same position and do not turn)
42 months	Pronated position (scissors pointing down towards table) no longer used
48 months	Can open/close scissors without extending pinky and ring finger (curls fingers)
	Cuts three-inch shapes with straight sides (square/triangle) within ½ inch of line
60 months	Cuts three inch shapes with curves or sharp angles within ¼ inch of line
66 months	Dynamic bilateral integration (both the scissors hand and paper hand turn to change direction)
72 months	Cuts complex shapes or paper toys guiding the paper to within ⅛ inch of all lines

- Use the words "open" and "close" to cue the child.

- Try using scissors that open automatically such as Fiskars first scissors, or loop scissors.

- Try snipping thick paper, foamboard, or snakes made out of playdough. The added resistance of these materials may help the child to feel the correct movements.

- Try using tiny scissors (ask your therapist where to order) because these require smaller movements than typical classroom scissors.

- Teach the child to put thumb in the small loop and middle and ring fingers in the other loop, with the index finger curled over the loop to provide support.

- Try wrapping the loops of scissors with foam or tape so they do not fully close. This may help the child to make shorter, more controlled cutting movements.

Poor arm position

Many children with delays in learning to hold the scissors have difficulty learning how to position their arms so that cutting will be efficient. Especially in the presence of low tone, the child may turn his or her arm so that the thumb is pointing down towards the table, instead of pointing up towards the ceiling with the cutting blades perpendicular to the paper. This is a very inefficient position, and may be helped by the following strategies:

- Teach the child to physically rest the arm on the table when cutting. Try using a mousepad or other tactile cue as a reminder.

- Gently press the elbow down and in towards the body as the child is cutting; this helps to provide a touch cue to keep the arm in the correct position.

- Practice other games that position the arm in a "thumbs-up" position. For example, holding a paddle and bouncing a ping-pong ball on the surface, or having relay races while holding a spoon that is cradling a tennis ball.

Difficulty guiding the paper to stay on the line

- Glue several large shapes or targets on a piece of paper. Have the child cut to a particular shape.

- Make "paths" that have a tactile cue, such as rows of dots made with a hole-punch, or trails of hardened glue, or wikki-stix.

- Cut out shapes (two each) using firm cardboard. Place a piece of paper between the two shapes, and have the child hold it like a sandwich and cut around the cardboard.

Visual perception skills

Visual perception refers to the brain's ability to understand what is seen, and is commonly immature in children with coordination difficulties. Children with visual perception problems have trouble recognizing, remembering, and organizing visual images as needed to understand written and pictorial symbols. This can interfere with many aspects of daily living, most notably learning to read, write, and learn math. A number of different types of perceptual skill can be affected. Although some professionals believe that perception is a basic psychological process that cannot be changed given therapy, others have found that children can be helped to attend better to the visual details of their world and of visually formatted learning material. The following are suggested strategies for helping children to develop visual perception skills.

Visual discrimination (the ability to recognize similarities and differences)

- Practice sorting objects by shape, color, size, or other attribute.
- For size discrimination, practice nesting cups or dolls.
- String beads according to color or shape sequence on a picture.
- Show the child a geometric form and identify all similar shapes in the room (e.g. rectangle = window, tabletop, light switch cover; circle = clock, face, ball, wheels).
- Color or shape bingo games.
- Look through colorful magazines to find objects that share certain attributes, e.g. all the "tall things," or all the "orange things."
- Use your finger to trace a letter or shape on the child's back and have the child guess what it is.

Spatial relations (perceiving the position of two or more objects in relation to one another)

- Copying block design patterns (parquetry or other design blocks).
- Copying pegboard designs from a simple picture.
- Dot-to-dot pictures.
- Mazes.
- Following a simple map.
- Crafts that involve copying from sequential instructions.

Visual memory (recalling a previous visual experience)

- Show two objects, have the child close his or her eyes, and remove one object. The child must identify what is missing. Gradually increase the number of items.
- Show two items, have the child close his or her eyes, remove *all* items, and ask the child to recall.

- Draw a design, cover it up, have the child copy the design from memory.

- Line up objects or toys on the table. Have the child close eyes while you shift the order of the objects. The child must reproduce the original order.

- Cup game. Find three identical cups, place an object under one, and move the position of the cups. The child must remember which cup hides the object.

Figure ground discrimination (attending to visual detail in a distracting background)

- "Hidden Picture" or "What's Wrong" puzzles.

- Go on a treasure hunt in a "busy" room and find a list of tiny objects that have been hidden.

- Jigsaw puzzles.

- Clip a section of print from a magazine or newspaper. Have the child circle all the words that begin or end with a targeted letter or letter combination (all the "b" words or all the words that end in "s").

Organizational skills

Many children with coordination difficulties are extremely disorganized in the way they manage their classroom activities. Difficulty understanding concepts related to time and space make it hard to organize a desk or backpack, complete assignments within the allotted time, or understand a class schedule. Difficulties with memory make it hard to follow classroom rules and routines, to remember homework assignments, or to apply learning strategies that have been reviewed in class. Children with organizational difficulties can be very perplexing to parents and teachers, because they are often bright and may be able to verbally articulate the appropriate rules, strategies or routines, but cannot put what they know into practice on a consistent basis. The following suggestions may be helpful for students with these problems.

Improving daily organization

- Teach the student to prepare for school the night before. Create a checklist that helps the student to plan what he or she will wear, check to see that homework is completed, and pack the backpack with necessary items.

- Provide a daily schedule for the student to review and refer to throughout the day. Designate a person (adult or peer) to help the student review his or her schedule at designated checkpoints throughout the day.

- Teach the student to organize his or her desk so that materials are placed in the same location each time they are put away. If necessary, prepare a simple diagram to provide visual reference. Use color-coded folders to help sort papers into various subject areas.

- Establish daily routines, such as cleaning out the backpack, with clear, concise rules (e.g. first, things to take home and give to parents; second, things to put away or throw away; third, things that require action and must be returned to school).

- In the classroom, post charts that visually outline expected classroom rules and procedures (e.g. at start of day, before you go home, etc.).

- Provide checklists for the student to self check assignment completion.

- Provide advance warning when routines must be disrupted or changed.

- Assist the student to develop plans of how he or she will complete long-term assignments, with a schedule for completion of small steps needed to reach the goal.

- Leave time at the end of the day for organizing materials and checking to see if homework assignments are clearly understood.

Compensating for problems with memory

- Provide step-by-step instructions, and have the student repeat each step so that you know he or she understands.

- Use teaching strategies that include "hands-on" approaches or that reflect a student's personal experiences. This is more effective for students with memory weaknesses than rote learning of facts.

- Allow calculators, spell checkers, digital watches, and other "quick reference" materials for students who need them.

- Teach mnemonics or acronyms to support memory.

- Teach the child to make notes and schedules as reminders of things to do.

- Provide frequent re-teaching of important concepts. Children with memory problems need much practice and repetition before they truly learn new skills. They need to "overlearn" new material.

- Avoid giving directions if the student's attention is not fully focused on you.

Chapter 7

THE SOCIAL IMPACT OF COORDINATION DIFFICULTIES

Fostering Self Esteem

Children with poor motor skills vary widely in their ability to cope with the social demands of home, school, and friendships. Some may easily take these differences in their stride. Rather than allowing problems with frustration or poor self esteem to interfere with social interactions, they find it natural to gravitate toward social activities that allow them to feel successful, and to behave in ways that lead them to be well accepted by others. Other children find this a daunting task. Problems with inattention or self regulation may trigger emotional outbursts during times of stress. The inability to compete with peers in sports or games involving physical skill may result in teasing or unacceptance. Just imagine how discouraging it must feel to always be the last player chosen for a team! Well-meaning teachers may, by frequently checking the student's work and making helpful comments, inadvertently draw attention to the fact that he or she is unable to do the work at the same level as other students. In an effort to avoid embarrassment, teachers may avoid displaying the student's artwork or special writing projects because the quality looks so different from that of other students. Imagine how frustrating it must be for a student to never have anything 'special' placed on display! Not surprisingly, several research studies have suggested that problems with emotional well-being are found more frequently among children with poor motor skill than with those who are more coordinated (Cratty 1994; Henderson, May and Umney 1989; Henderson and Hall 1982; VanRossum and Vermeer 1990). Table 7.1 lists behaviors that might suggest the presence of poor social coping abilities in the child.

The first step in helping the child with coordination difficulties to develop a positive attitude is for parents, teachers, and all others who have close contact with the child to learn all they can about the child's strengths, weaknesses, temperament,

Table 7.1 Behavioral indications of poor social coping skills

- Frequent tantrums or arguments
- Difficulty making friends
- Lack of reciprocity in conversation
- Excessive competition during games or sports
- Difficulty noticing and responding to the needs and interests of others
- Inflexibility towards how rules are followed or interpreted
- Showing aggression towards others
- Acting silly to draw attention away from performance difficulties
- Overt avoidance of school or other group activities

and individual learning style. With this knowledge, adults can begin to appreciate difficulties the child may experience, anticipate situations that have the potential to cause stress, and develop more realistic expectations for the child's performance and behavior in challenging situations. It is easy for an adult to think that the child who chooses not to engage in competitive sports is "cowardly" until they appreciate that problems with low tone, poor physical endurance, and poor motor planning make these activities a highly unpleasant experience. Or, they may think the child who never invites friends over is "lazy" or "inconsiderate," until they realize that problems with understanding social conventions or poor conversational skills may cause intense anxiety for the child in social situations.

It is important for adults to accept the child for who he or she is, and to avoid imposing their own expectations on the child, or expressing disappointment in the shortcomings of the child. If the child is a member of a family that places high value on competitive sports, but does not enjoy these activities or cannot succeed, find some other activity that the child enjoys and is successful with, and celebrate the child's participation in something that makes him feel good about himself! The following are strategies for creating a positive emotional bond with the child, and helping him or her to cope with the emotional consequences of coordination difficulties:

- Try to anticipate situations that may cause emotional stress, and either avoid these if possible or help the child to prepare for the stress by discussing possible problems and strategies for coping. Carol Gray (2000) has developed a model for helping children to write and rehearse Social Stories™ that teach them how to behave and react to frequently occurring situations that are hard for them. This strategy can be easily incorporated into home or school, and is very helpful for some children.

- Use reflective listening to understand the child's feelings. Comments like "I know you get kind of scared when you get together with friends because you sometimes have a hard time sharing" are phrased in a non judgmental manner, yet let the child know that you understand his or her feelings.

- Develop a style of sharing your own personal challenges and how you cope with them, so the child learns that he or she is not the only one in the world who has to cope with stressful situations.

- Try to be understanding, and not impatient, when the child makes mistakes.

- Celebrate the child's strengths and efforts. If the child is trying really hard to learn to throw a baseball yet is failing miserably, find something to praise with comments like "I like the way you are trying!" or "You're getting closer!"

- Encourage the child to participate in sports that incorporate the child's strengths, allow success, and are fun for the child. Bowling, martial arts, gymnastics, and swimming are examples of athletic activities that seem easier for some children with motor difficulties, or for those who struggle with social situations. Look for coaches who are patient and who try to promote the personal development of each child, instead of those who only draw attention to the "best" performers on the team. Explain to coaches that the child may need advance notice of changes in schedule or routine, needs to have choices whenever possible, and may have trouble responding to feedback that is called out to the field instead of being spoken clearly and concisely face to face.

- Behavior plans or strategies that are in place for home and school should be carried over to extracurricular activities if at all possible so that the child does not receive different messages about his or her behavior in different environments.

- Observe closely to notice when the child behaves in a positive social manner, and offer praise when you "catch them being good."

- Build structure and routine into the child's day, and give as much notice as possible if routines need to be disrupted. In this way, he or she will be better able to anticipate those situations that may cause distress.

- Find local organizations that might offer appropriate peer interactions, such as scout troops or local recreation programs. Share information

about the child's difficulties, and look for leaders that seem supportive
and able to cope with a child who is "different."

- Consider setting up "play dates" or other pre-arranged social activities
to help the child make friends. And don't be afraid to use subtle bribery
in the form of a special activity (e.g. a trip to the zoo) or reward (e.g. a
special food treat) to help other children want to participate and enjoy
the experience.

- Consider seeking outside help for developing social skills if the child is
really struggling. Most schools have guidance counselors who can
provide direct training in social skills or in developing and maintaining
friendships, or who can refer to private professionals if indicated.

Coping with teasing and bullying

Teasing is a normal part of childhood, and generally begins around the age of four
or five when children first begin to notice the differences between themselves and
others. Teasing often begins innocently enough as children make comments about
the differences they observe, usually physical traits such as gender, skin color, or
size. Many children make these comments out of their own insecurity as they try to
reassure themselves that their own differences are, in fact, okay. Children who send
out signals to others that they lack self confidence, such as children with coordination or social communication problems, are especially vulnerable to teasing and
bullying. Some bullies act out of their own insecurities, and pick on children who
remind them of their own vulnerabilities. Others act out of a need to be in control.
They actually derive pleasure from inflicting suffering on others, and lack empathy
for the feelings of others. Bullying affects as many as two in five children at some
point during their school years. It tends to gradually increase during the elementary
years, peaks in middle school, and gradually declines in high school.

Bullying can take several forms. Nonphysical bullying includes name-calling,
threatening, exclusion from social activities, talking behind the child's back, and
other behaviors that can cause significant emotional stigma. Physical bullying can
include spitting, kicking, pushing, hitting, stealing, or damaging personal belong-
ings. It may seem that physical bullying is more serious than nonphysical bullying,
but both can cause serious psychological trauma to the child.

Unfortunately, some children fail to let adults know that they are being teased
or bullied. Very young children may not even understand that certain behaviors are
unacceptable. Older children may be reluctant to let adults know they are being
bullied for a variety of reasons. A child with poor body image or low self esteem
may actually believe that he or she deserves to be bullied. Others hope that the

problem will just "go away," or they may keep silence out of fear that bringing the matter to the attention of adults will make the bullies angrier and more aggressive. Some children are fearful that telling a parent about bullying may cause the parent to get angry or upset, or to take action that the child might find embarrassing.

The following signs suggest that a child might be experiencing teasing or bullying from his or her peers:

- unexplained cuts or bruises, torn clothes, lost or broken toys
- avoidance of school or recreational pastimes
- frequent complaints of headaches or stomach aches that quickly disappear
- avoiding having friends come to the house
- changes in eating or sleeping habits
- oversensitivity to criticism
- mood changes (depression, anxiety, aggression).

Many schools have effectively implemented anti-bullying programs. The features of these programs typically stress the importance of respecting oneself, speaking up when bullying is observed, and learning how to divert attention away from children who are engaged in bullying behaviors.

Parents of children who are known or suspected victims of bullying may find themselves outraged by the situation. It is easy to want to take the matter in hand in an effort to prevent the child from emotional distress. It is far better, however, to react calmly and to partner with the child to teach him or her coping strategies that can be used throughout life. Certainly, serious behaviors such as those that involve stalking, physical abuse, or stealing are actually criminal in nature, and should be brought to the attention of school officials (when they occur in school) or to the police (if they occur outside school). It is generally not a good idea to confront the parents of the bully or bullies, unless you know them well enough to predict their reaction and to feel certain that you will be able to work together towards a solution. The following are suggestions for helping the child who is a victim of teasing or bullying:

- Encourage the child to participate in activities that build on his or her strengths. This is a way to build self esteem, and may also expose the child to new friends who share similar interests and talents.

- Encourage the child to talk about being bullied, and to trust that you will take no action without the child's knowledge. Reassure the child that he or she is not at fault, that the hurtful statements are not true, and that bullying is always unacceptable.

- Increase supervision of the child's activities and whereabouts to become more aware of potential problems.

- Teach the child specific strategies for coping with teasing. These might include avoiding the teaser (make no eye contact, walk away); using an "I" message (e.g. "I don't like it when you say something like that"); accepting the comments in a positive tone (e.g. "You're right, I'm not very good at throwing a ball, am I?," or "Thanks for letting me know!"); laughing or smiling in response to hurtful words; asking an adult to intervene.

- Talk to the child about situations in your own life that have caused distress, and model how you have handled conflicts.

- Consider counseling if the child is unable to cope given parent support.

References

Cratty, B.J. (1994). "Social and emotional accompaniments to poor motor coordination." In *Clumsy Child Syndromes: Descriptions, Evaluation and Remediation* (pp.253–271). Chur, Switzerland: Harwood Academic Publishers.

Gray, C. (2000) *The New Social Story Book — Illustrated Edition.* Arlington, TX: Future Horizons, Inc.

Henderson, S.E., May, D.S. and Umney, M. (1989). "An exploratory study of goal-setting behavior, self-concept and locus of control in children with movement difficulties." *European Journal of Special Needs 4*, 1–4.

Henderson, S.E. and Hall, D. (1982). "Concomitants of clumsiness in young school children." *Developmental Medicine and Child Neurology 24*, 448–460.

VanRossum, J.H.A. and Vermeer, A. (1990). "Perceived competence: A validation study in the field of motoric remedial teaching." *International Journal of Disability, Development, and Maturation 37*, 71–81.

GLOSSARY

Accessibility plan: An individualized program of instruction for students with disabilities as provided for by the UK Special Educational Needs and Disability Act 2001.

Apraxia: Inability to plan and carry out unfamiliar motor activities in a coordinated manner. A more serious type of motor planning disorder than that seen with developmental coordination disorder, often occurring as a result of acquired brain injury.

Articulation: The ability to coordinate the mouth, tongue and lips to produce sounds used in speech.

Asperger's syndrome: A neurological disorder, thought to be a mild form of autism, that typically involves normal intelligence, but difficulty with social skills, conversational speech, and motor coordination.

Attention deficit disorder (ADD): A neurological disorder characterized by significant and persistent inattention and impulsivity that impact upon learning and social behaviors. When excessive motor restlessness or fidgeting co-exist, it is known as attention deficit hyperactivity disorder (ADHD).

Autism: A neurological disorder, usually identified within the first three years of life, that seriously impacts development with impairments in the areas of sensory processing, language development, and social interaction.

Bilateral integration: The neurological process of organizing sensations from both sides of the body to allow coordinated movements between the two body sides.

Body awareness: An unconscious awareness of one's body parts, and how they move and interact with one another.

Cerebral palsy: A nonprogressive disorder of movement and posture that results from damage to the brain occuring within the first three years of life.

Chaining: A behavioral training technique that involves breaking down a task into its component steps, then teaching them one at a time starting with either the first step in the sequence (*forward chaining*) or the last step in the sequence (*backward chaining*).

Childhood apraxia of speech (CAS): Difficulty or inability to initiate and produce nonspeech or speech movements.

Complementary and alternative medicine (CAM): Various health systems, practices, and interventions that are not considered to be part of conventional medicine, often because they lack rigorous scientific evidence for their safety and efficiency.

Core trunk strength: The ability of the trunk (middle part of the body) to support posture against gravity, maintain balance, and provide a base of support for head, arm, and leg movement.

Cortical: Relating to the cortex (grey matter) of the brain.

Developmental coordination disorder (DCD): A developmental disorder that includes a marked impairment of motor coordination, not associated with any medical condition, that significantly interferes with academic learning or with performance of activities of daily living.

Developmental milestones: Skills that most children can be expected to achieve at a predictable age, for example understanding "no" at eight to nine months of age, and taking a first step at 11–13 months of age. Children with developmental delays achieve milestones later than children with typical development.

Developmental verbal dyspraxia: See *childhood apraxia of speech*.

Distal: Pertaining to parts of the body that are far away from the midline or the trunk.

Dyspraxia: Limited ability to plan and carry out unfamiliar motor activities in a coordinated manner. Also called poor motor planning. See *developmental coordination disorder*.

Extension: A movement that causes a joint to straighten.

Flexion: A movement that causes a joint to bend.

Functional vision impairments: Visual impairments that are the result of problems that cause the eyes to function inefficiently. See *refractive errors of vision*; *visual efficiency disorders*.

Hypertonia: Increased muscle tone; increased resistance to passive movement of a limb.

Hypotonia: Decreased muscle tone; decreased resistance to passive movement of a limb.

Ideation: The mental ability to conceptualize a motor goal and formulate an idea of how to accomplish that goal; one aspect of motor planning.

Individualized educational program (IEP): A written plan, mandated by US federal law, that specifies the services, supports, goals and objectives for any student who requires special education services.

Kinesthesia: Knowledge of joint position and body movement in space, without the use of vision—for example, being able to write your name in the air with your eyes closed.

Motor planning: See *praxis*.

Muscle tone: The degree of tension present in muscles when at rest or when passively moved, which may range from low to high. Children with low muscle tone typically have poor posture and increased joint mobility, while children with high tone may have stiff movements and limited flexibility.

Oral apraxia: Difficulty with volitional control of nonspeech movements.

Pervasive developmental disorder: A severe developmental disability, related to autism, that includes impaired sensory processing skills, poor communication and social skills, and varying levels of learning and behavior difficulties.

Placebo effect: The perception that an intervention has caused positive change, when those changes could be attributed to other factors.

Positive reinforcement: The use of rewards or praise to increase desired behaviors.

Praxis: Also called motor planning. The ability to plan, organize, sequence, and execute unfamiliar motor activities in a skillful manner.

Prone: Lying face down.

Proprioception: The unconscious sensation of body position that comes from sensory receptors in the joints, muscles and tendons.

Proximal: Pertaining to parts of the body that are close to the midline or the trunk.

Radial: Pertaining to the side of the hand closest to the thumb.

Reflex: An automatic, unplanned motor response to a sensory input.

Refractive errors of vision: Problems with how light is focused on the retina of the eye, including nearsightedness (difficulty seeing things far away), farsightedness (difficulty seeing things close up) and astigmatism (blurred vision at near and far points).

Sensory defensiveness: A tendency to over-react to sensory experiences that others would find harmless.

Sensory integration: The organization of sensory input in order to make an adaptive response for learning or behaving.

Sensory modulation: The ability to use sensory input from the body and the environment in such a way as to maintain an appropriate level of arousal, attention, and self-organization.

Sensory perception: The ability of the brain to interpret sensations.

Sensory reception: The process by which a sensory organ (e.g. eyes, ears, skin) transmits information to the brain (sight, sound, touch).

Soft neurologic signs: Neurological characteristics, such as motor overflow or mixed dominance, that are normal in young children but suggest immature development of the central nervous system when identified in older children.

Spasticity: Abnormally increased muscle tone.

Structural vision problems: Vision disorders that relate to the structure or health of the eyes and their related structures. Anophthalmia (congenital absence of the eyeball), cataracts, and glaucoma are some examples of structural vision problems.

Supine: Lying face up.

Tactile defensiveness: A type of sensory defensiveness that causes excessive emotional reactions, hyperactivity, or other behavior problems in response to certain types of tactile experiences.

Ulnar: Pertaining to the side of the hand closest to the pinky finger.

Verbal apraxia: Difficulty with volitional movements for speech production.

Vestibular system: The sensory system, located within the inner ear, that provides information about gravity, body movement within space, and head position. This sense plays an important role in balance and in coordinated movements of the eyes and body.

Visual efficiency disorders: Problems with using smooth, well- coordinated muscle control that allows the eyes to gather necessary visual information. These problems can result in poor attention to visual detail, losing one's place, avoidance of visually challenging work, and eyestrain.

Appendix I

TESTS AND ASSESSMENT TOOLS

Fine and gross motor skills

Bruinninks-Oseretsky Test of Motor Proficiency II
Publisher: AGS Publishing/Pearson Assessment

- Age range 4–21 years.

- Testing time approximately 45–60 minutes for full battery, or 15–20 minutes for short form.

- Eight subtests assess: fine motor precision, fine motor integration, manual dexterity, bilateral coordination, balance, running speed and agility, upper-limb coordination, and strength.

- Clinical validity for high-functioning autism, Asperger's syndrome, DCD.

Movement Assessment Battery for Children
Publisher: Harcourt Assessment (England)

- Age range 4–12 years.

- Testing time 20–30 minutes.

- Assessment battery consisting of three components: classroom assessment of movement problems and screening of at-risk students; comprehensive assessment of movement competence; guidelines for a cognitive-motor approach to intervention.

Peabody Developmental Motor Scales — 2
Publisher: Pro-Ed

- Age range birth to six years.

- Testing time approximately 45–60 minutes.

- Motor development test including gross motor (reflexes, stationary balance, locomotion) and fine motor (object manipulation, grasping, visual-motor integration).

Test of Gross Motor Development — Second Edition
Publisher: Pro-Ed

- Age range 3–10.11 years.

- Testing time approximately 15–20 minutes.

- Identifies students who are significantly below peers in gross motor development.

- Includes two subtests, each measuring six skills: locomotor (run, gallop, hop, leap, horizontal jump, slide) and object control (striking a stationary ball, stationary dribble, kick, catch, overhand throw, underhand roll).

Toddler and Infant Motor Evaluation (TIME)
Publisher: Harcourt Assessment Inc.

- Age range birth to 3.6 years.

- Testing time approximately 15–45 minutes.

- Designed to measure the quality of movement in infants and toddlers with atypical motor development, and the relationship of motor ability to functional performance.

Handwriting

Children's Handwriting Evaluation Scale (CHES)
Children's Handwriting Evaluation Scale-Manuscript (CHES-M)
Publisher: Texas Scottish Rite Hospital

- Age range grades 1–2 (CHES-M) and 3–8 (CHES).

- Testing time approximately 10 minutes.

- Brief, norm-referenced writing test that measures the quality and rate of handwriting when copying a standard sample of text that incorporates most letters of the alphabet.

Evaluation Tool of Children's Handwriting (ETCH)
Publisher: Pocket Full of Therapy

- Age range grades 1–6.

- Testing time approximately 20–30 minutes.

- Subtests in alphabet writing, numeral writing, near-point copying, far-point copying, manuscript-to-cursive transition, dictation, and sentence composition.

- Scores include word and letter legibility percentages, speed (letters per minute) and qualitative measures of the biomechanical aspects of writing.

Minnesota Handwriting Test
Publisher: Harcourt Assessment Inc.

- Age range mid-first grade through second grade.

- Testing time less than five minutes.

- Individual or group administration.

- Norm-referenced test that assesses manuscript and D'Nealian handwriting.

- Assesses rate of handwriting as well as five quality areas: legibility, form, alignment, size, and spacing.

The Print Tool
Publisher: Handwriting Without Tears

- Age range six and older.

- Testing time approximately 15 minutes.

- Can be used for any handwriting curriculum.

- Assesses memory, orientation, placement, size, start, sequence, control, and spacing of uppercase letters, lowercase letters, and numbers.

- Assessment results are linked to specific remediation strategies.

Shore Handwriting Screening
Publisher: Pro-Ed

- Age range 3–7 years.

- Testing time approximately 15–20 minutes.

- Screening tool designed to evaluate postural control, hand control, letter and number formation, and environmental focus.

Test of Handwriting Skill
Publisher: Psychological and Educational Publications, Inc.

- Age range 5.0–10.11 years.

- Testing time approximately 15–20 minutes.

- Individual or group administration.

- Norm-referenced test that measures how well children can write letters, numbers, or words spontaneously, from dictation, and from copying. It also measures speed of writing letters spontaneously.

Screening and school function tests

Clinical Observations of Motor and Postural Skills — Second Edition (COMPS-2)
Publisher: Pro-Ed

- Age range 5–15 years.

- Testing time approximately 15–20 minutes.

- Uses six items (slow movements, rapid forearm rotation, finger–nose touching, prone extension posture, asymmetric tonic neck reflex, supine flexion posture) to screen for DCD.

Miller Assessment for Preschoolers (MAP)
Publisher: PsychCorp/Harcourt Assessment Inc.

- Age range 2.9–5.8 years.

- Testing time approximately 30 minutes.

- Screening test that gives scores in five areas: foundations (sensory and motor maturity), coordination (fine, gross and oral-motor), verbal (expressive and receptive language, auditory memory), nonverbal (visual perception, memory, and spatial organization), and complex tasks (combined sensory, motor, and cognitive tasks).

Miller Function and Assessment Scales
Publisher: PsychCorp/Harcourt Assessment Inc.

- Age range 2.6–7.11 years.

- Testing time 55–65 minutes.

- Assesses fine, gross, and visual-motor skills critical to classroom performance.

- Appropriate for children with mild to severe motor difficulties.

Quick Neurological Screening Test — II
Publisher: Academic Therapy Publications

- Age range 5–18 years.

- Testing time approximately 20 minutes.

- Used as a screening device to identify children who have possible learning disabilities.

School Function Assessment (SFA)
Publisher: Harcourt Assessment, Inc.

- Age range kindergarten to sixth grade.

- Testing time variable: ratings completed by school personnel familiar with the child. Individual scales may be completed in as little as 10 minutes.

- Monitors a student's participation in school activities, as well as typical supports and adaptations needed.

Sensory processing and sensory integration

DeGangi-Berk Test of Sensory Integration
Publisher: Western Psychological Services

- Age range 3–5 years.

- Testing time approximately 30 minutes.

- Criterion-referenced screening test including measures of postural control, bilateral motor coordination, and reflex integration.

Infant/Toddler Symptom Checklist
Publisher: Harcourt Assessment, Inc.

- Age range 7–30 months.

- Testing time approximately 10 minutes.

- Symptom checklist designed to screen for sensory and regulatory disorders; helps to determine if a child is predisposed to having problems with sensory integration.

Sensory Integration and Praxis Tests (SIPT)
Publisher: Western Psychological Services

- Age range 4.0–8.11 years.

- Testing time approximately two hours.

- Provides a comprehensive assessment of sensory processing and motor planning ability.

- Requires certification to administer.

Sensory Profile
Publisher: PsychCorp/Harcourt Assessment Inc.

- Several versions available for ages infant through adult, and for school settings.

- Judgement-based caregiver questionnaire that attempts to link sensory processing strengths and weaknesses with functional difficulties.

- Testing time variable: caregivers need 10–30 minutes to complete the questionnaire, depending on use of a long or short form. Compilation of scores requires 20–30 minutes.

Test of Sensory Functions in Infants (TSFI)
Publisher: Western Psychological Services

- Age range 4–18 months.

- Testing time approximately 20 minutes.

- Provides overall measure of sensory processing and reactivity in infants with difficult temperaments, developmental delays, and those at risk for learning disorders.

Speech apraxia and oral-motor problems

The Apraxia Profile
Publisher: PsychCorp

- Age range 2–12.

- Testing time 25–35 minutes.

- Designed for children with significant speech intelligibility deficits, this test assists in the differential diagnosis of developmental verbal apraxia and identifies the presence of oral apraxia.

KSPT: Kaufman Speech Praxis Test for Children
Publisher: Pro-Ed

- Age range 2.0–5.11 years.

- Testing time approximately 15 minutes.

- Designed to identify the level of breakdown in the child's ability to imitate the examiner's speech.

- Can be used to generate individualized education programs.

STDAS-2: Screening Test for Developmental Apraxia of Speech — Second Edition
Publisher: Pro-Ed

- Age range 4–12 years.

- Testing time approximately 15 minutes.

- Identifies both typical speech-language problems and associated oral problems.

- Contains four subtests, including expressive language discrepancy, prosody, verbal sequencing, and articulation.

Visual motor integration

Bender Visual-Motor Gestalt Test, Second Edition
Publisher: Riverside

- Age range three to adult.

- Testing time 5–10 minutes plus five minutes for supplemental tests.

- Brief assessment of visual-motor integration that includes simple supplemental tests of motor and perceptual skills as well as visual-motor memory.

Developmental Test of Visual-Motor Integration — Fifth Edition
Publisher: Pearson Assessment

- Age range 3–18 years.

- Testing time approximately 10–15 minutes.

- Assesses visual-motor performance through copying geometric designs with paper and pencil.

- Supplemental subtests evaluate the relative contributions of visual perception and motor coordination to test results.

Full Range Test of Visual-Motor Integration (FRTVMI)
Publisher: Pro-Ed

- Age range 5–74 years.

- Testing time 15–30 minutes.

- Assesses visual-motor integration across the lifespan through copying of geometric figures that increase in complexity.

Preschool Visual Motor Assessment
Publisher: Therapro

- Age range 3.6–5.6 years.

- Testing time approximately 20 minutes.

- Includes two subtests: drawing and block patterns.

- Assesses perception of position in space, awareness of spatial relationships, color and shape discrimination, matching two attributes simultaneously, and the ability to reproduce what is seen.

Wide Range Assessment of Visual Motor Ability
Publisher: Psychological Assessment Resources, Inc.

- Age range 3–17 years.

- Testing time approximately 4–10 minutes each for three subtests (drawing, matching, pegboard).

- Allows assessment and comparison of visual-spatial, fine motor, and integrated visual motor skills.

Visual perception and functional vision skills

Developmental Test of Visual Perception — Second Edition
Publisher: Pro-Ed

- Age range 4–10 years.

- Testing time approximately 45 minutes.

- Includes eight subtests: eye–hand coordination, position in space, copying, figure–ground, spatial relations, visual closure, visual-motor speed, form constancy.

McDowell Vision Screening Test
Publisher: Slosson Educational Publications

- Age range 2.9–5.4 years.

- Testing time 10–20 minutes.

- Behavioral assessment of visual performance in five areas: distance visual acuity, near-point visual acuity, ocular alignment and motility, color perception, and ocular function.

Motor Free Visual Perception Test (MVPT) — Third Edition
Publisher: Academic Therapy Publications

- Age range 4–85 years.

- Testing time approximately 20 minutes.

- Provides a general measure of visual perceptual performance while avoiding a motor response.

Test of Visual Perceptual Skills — Non-Motor (TVPS) — Third Edition
Publisher: Psychological and Educational Publications, Inc.

- Age range 4–19 years.

- Testing time approximately 30–40 minutes.

- Identifies strengths and weaknesses in visual perceptual performance in a nonmotor format.

- Provides an overall score as well as subtest scores in the following areas: visual discrimination, visual memory, visual spatial relationships, visual form constancy, visual sequential memory, visual figure–ground, and visual closure.

Visual Skills Appraisal
Publisher: Academic Therapy Publications

- Age range 5–9 years; can be used to screen older children.

- Testing time approximately 10–15 minutes.

- Screening test that measures eye pursuits, scanning, alignment, locating movements, eye–hand coordination, and fixation unity.

- Offers cut-off scores indicating the need for formal evaluation, and suggested activities to strengthen visual skills.

Appendix II

RECOMMENDED READING

(Books and articles marked with * are especially suitable for a nonprofessional audience.)

Assessment

Amundsen, S.J.C. (1992) "Handwriting: Evaluation and Intervention in School Settings." In J.C. Smith and C. Pehoski (eds) *Development of Hand Skills in the Child* (pp.63–78) Rockville, MD: American Occupational Therapy Association.

Asher, I.E. (1996) *Occupational Therapy Assessment Tools: An Annotated Index, Second Edition*. Bethesda, MD: American Occupational Therapy Association.

Cammisa, K. (1991) "Testing difficult children for sensory integrative dysfunction." *Sensory Integration Special Interest Section Newsletter 14*, 2, 1–4.

Carrasco, R.C. (1993) "Key components of sensory integration evaluation." *Sensory Integration Special Interest Section Newsletter 16*, 2, 1–2.

King-Thomas, L. and Hacker, B. (1987) *A Therapist's Guide to Pediatric Assessment*. Boston, MA: Little, Brown and Co.

* Lyman, H.B. (1997) *Test Scores and What They Mean, Sixth Edition*. Boston, MA: Allyn and Bacon.

Radcliffe, J. and Moss, E.M. (1996) "Guidelines for Use of Tests in Pediatrics." In L.A. Kurtz, P.W. Dowrick, S.E. Levy and M.L. Batshaw (Eds) *Handbook of Developmental Disabilities: Resources for Interdisciplinary Care* (pp.152–159) Gaithersburg, MD: Aspen.

Tseng, M.H. and Cermak, S. (1991) "The evaluation of handwriting in children." *Sensory Integration Quarterly XIX*, 4, 1–6.

Behavior management

Blechman, E. (1985) *Solving Child Behavior Problems at Home and School*. Champaign, IL: Research Press.

* Forehand, R. and Long, N. (1996) *Parenting the Strong-Willed Child*. Chicago, IL: Contemporary Books.

*Greene, R.W. (2001) *The Explosive Child, Second Edition*. New York, NY: HarperCollins.

* Greenspan, S.I. (1995) *The Challenging Child: Understanding, Raising, and Enjoying the Five "Difficult" Types of Children*. Reading, MA: Addison-Wesley.

Martin, G. and Pears, J. (1992) *Behavior Modification: What it is and How to do it*. Englewood Cliffs, NJ: Prentice-Hall.

* Phelan, T.W. (2003) *1–2–3 Magic: Effective Discipline for Children 2–12, Third Edition*. Glen Ellyn, IL: ParentMagic, Inc.

Phelan, T.W. and Schonour, S.J. (2004) *1–2–3 Magic for Teachers*. Glen Ellyn, IL: ParentMagic, Inc.

* Simons, L. (2000) *Taking "No" for an Answer and Other Skills Children Need*. Seattle, WA: Parenting Press, Inc.

Complementary and alternative approaches

Alecson, D.G. (1999) *Alternative Treatments for Children within the Autism Spectrum: Effective, Natural Solutions for Learning Disorders, Attention Deficits, and Autistic Behaviors*. Los Angeles, CA: Keats Publishing.

Brue, A.W. and Oakland, T.D. (2002) "Alternative treatments for attention deficit/hyperactivity disorders: Does evidence support their use?" *International Journal of Integrative Medicine 4*, 4, 28–30, 32–35.

Charman, R.A. (2000) *Complementary Therapies for Physical Therapists*. Oxford: Boston: Butterworth-Heineman.

* Chivers, M. (2006) *Dyslexia and Alternative Therapies*. London: Jessica Kingsley Publishers.

* Dillard, J. and Ziporin, T. (1998) *Alternative Medicine for Dummies*. Foster City, CA: IDG Books.

* Grant, C. and Briggs, M. (1999) *ADD and ADHD: Complementary Solutions*. Essential Research Solutions, Inc.

Jacobson, J.W., Foxx, R.M. and Mulick, J.A. (eds) (2005) *Controversial Therapies for Developmental Disabilities: Fad, Fashion and Science in Professional Practice*. Mahwah, NJ: Erlbaum.

Nickel, R.E. (1996) "Controversial therapies for young children with developmental disabilities." *Infants and Young Children 8*, 4, 29–40.

Handwriting and hand function

* Alston, J. and Taylor, J. (2000) *Teaching Handwriting: A Guide for Teachers and Parents*. Stafford, UK: QEd Publications, Ltd.

Benbow, M., Hanft, B. and Marsh, D. (1992) "Handwriting in the Classroom: Improving Written Communication." In C. Royeen (ed.) *AOTA Self-Study Series: Classroom Applications for School Based Practice (Lesson IV)* Rockville, MD: American Occupational Therapy Association, Inc.

Case-Smith, J. and Pehoski, C. (eds) (1992) *Development of Hand Skills in the Child*. Rockville, MD: The American Occupational Therapy Association, Inc.

* Cavey, D.W. (2000) *Dysgraphia: Why Johnny Can't Write*. Austin, TX: Pro-Ed.

Cornhill, H. and Case-Smith, J. (1996) "Factors that relate to good and poor handwriting." *The American Journal of Occupational Therapy 50*, 9, 732–739.

Dornau, G. and Taylor, J. (2005) *Which Handwriting Scheme?* Stafford, UK: QEd Publications, Ltd.

Henderson, A. and Pehoski, C. (eds) (2005) *Hand Function in the Child: Foundations for Remediation, Second Edition*. St. Louis, MO: Elsevier Health Sciences.

Kranowitz, C.S. (2003) *The Out-of-Sync Child has Fun: Activities for Kids with Sensory Integrative Dysfunction*. New York, NY: Perigee Trade.

* Kurtz, L.A. (1994) "Helpful handwriting hints." *Teaching Exceptional Children* 58–59.

* Landy, J.M. and Burridge, K.R. (2000) *Ready-to-Use Fine Motor Skills and Handwriting Activities for Young Children*. Hillsborough, OR: Center for Applied Research in Education.

* Lear, R. (1999) *Fingers and Thumbs: Toys and Activities for Children with Hand Problems*. St Louis, MO: Elsevier Health Sciences.

Maeland, A.E. (1992) "Handwriting and perceptual motor skills in clumsy, dysgraphic, and normal children." *Perceptual and Motor Skills 75*, 1207–1217.

McHale, K. and Cermak, S. (1992) "Fine motor activities in elementary school: Preliminary findings and provisional implications for children with fine motor problems." *American Journal of Occupational Therapy 46*, 10, 898–903.

* Parker, J.N. and Parker, P.M. (eds) (2002) *The Official Parent's Sourcebook on Dysgraphia: A Revised and Updated Directory for the Internet Age*. San Diego, CA: Icon Health Publications.

Richards, R.G. (1998) *The Writing Dilemma: Understanding Dysgraphia*. Riverside, CA: Richards Educational Therapy Center, Inc.

Motor skills in dyspraxia, autism, ADHD, learning disabilities

* Barkley, R.A. (2000) *Taking Charge of ADHD: The Complete, Authoritative Guide for Parents, Revised Edition*. New York, NY: The Guilford Press.

Case-Smith, J. and Pehoski, C. (eds) (1992) *Development of Hand Skills in the Child*. Rockville, MD: American Occupational Therapy Association, Inc.

Cermak, S.A. and Larkin, D. (2002) *Developmental Coordination Disorder*. Albany, NY: Delmar.

Cratty, B.J. (1994) *Clumsy Child Syndromes: Descriptions, Evaluation and Remediation*. Langhorne, PA: Harwood Academic Publishers.

David, K.S. (1994) "Developmental Coordination Disorders." In S.K. Campbell (ed.) *Physical Therapy for Children* (pp.425–458) Philadelphia, PA: W.B. Saunders.

* Eckersley, J. (2004) *Coping with Dyspraxia*. London: Sheldon Press.

* Kirby, A. and Drew, S. (2003) *Guide to Dyspraxia and Developmental Coordination Disorders*. London: David Fulton Publishers.

Missiuna, C. (ed.) (2001) *Children with Developmental Coordination Disorder: Strategies for Success*. New York, The Haworth Press, Inc.

Missiuna, C. and Polatajko, H. (1995) "Developmental dyspraxia by any other name: Are they all just clumsy children?" *American Journal of Occupational Therapy 49*, 7, 619–627.

O'Brien, V., Cermak, S.A. and Murray, E. (1988) "The relationship between visual-perceptual motor abilities and clumsiness in children with and without learning disabilities." *American Journal of Occupational Therapy 42*, 6, 359–363.

Piaget, J. and Inhelder, B. (1969) *The Psychology of the Child*. New York, NY: Basic Books.

Powell, R.P. and Bishop, D.V. (1992) "Clumsiness and perceptual problems in children with specific language impairment." *Developmental Medicine and Child Neurology 34*, 9, 755–765.

Schoemaker, M.M., Hijlkema, M.G. and Kalverboer, A.F. (1994) "Physiotherapy for clumsy children: An evaluation study." *Developmental Medicine and Child Neurology 36*, 2, 143–155.

* Siegal, B. (2003) *Helping Children with Autism Learn: Treatment Approaches for Parents and Professionals*. New York, NY: Oxford University Press.

* Silver, L. (1998) *The Misunderstood Child: A Guide for Parents of Children with Learning Disabilities, Third Edition*. New York, NY: Three Rivers Press.

Sugden, D. and Chambers, M. (2005) *Children with Developmental Coordination Disorder*. London: John Wiley and Sons.

Wallen, M. and Walker, R. (1995) "Occupational therapy practice with children with perceptual motor dysfunction: Findings of a literature review and survey." *Australian Occupational Therapy Journal 42*, 1, 15–25.

Neurodevelopmental therapy

Bobath, K. and Bobath, B. (1984) "Neuro-developmental Treatment." In D. Scrutton (ed.) *Management of the Motor Disorders of Children with Cerebral Palsy: Clinics in Developmental Medicine* (No. 90, pp.6–18) Philadelphia, PA: J.B. Lippincott.

Duff, S. and Quinn, L. (2002) "Motor Learning and Motor Control." In D. Cech and S. Marin (eds) *Functional Movement Development Across the Life Span, Second Edition* (pp.86–117) Philadelphia, PA: W.B. Saunders.

Howle, J.M. (ed.) (2002) *Neuro-Developmental Treatment Approach: Theoretical Foundations and Principles of Clinical Practice*. Laguna Beach, CA: NDTA.

* Martin, S. (2006) *Teaching Motor Skills to Children with Cerebral Palsy and Similar Movement Disorders: A Guide for Parents and Professionals*. Bethesda, MD: Woodbine House.

Shumway-Cook, A. and Woolacott, M.H. (2000) *Motor Control: Theory and Practical Applications, Second Edition*. Philadelphia, PA: Lippincott, Williams and Wilkins.

School services

* Anderson, W. Chitwood, S. and Hayden, D. (1997) *Negotiating the Special Education Maze: A Guide for Parents and Teachers, 3rd Edition*. Rockville, MD: Woodbine House.

* Bissell, J., Fisher, J., Owens, C. and Polcyn, P. (1988) *Sensory Motor Handbook: A Guide for Implementing and Modifying Activities in the Classroom*. Torrance, CA: Sensory Integration International.

Dixon, G. and Addy, L.M. (2004) *Making Inclusion Work for Children with Dyspraxia*. London: Routledge.

Jones, N. (2005) *Developing School Provision for Children with Dyspraxia: A Practical Guide*. London: Paul Chapman Educational Publishing.

Levine, K.J. (1991) *Fine Motor Dysfunction: Therapeutic Strategies in the Classroom*. Tucson, AZ: Therapy Skill Builders.

Self-care skills

* Ball, M.F. (2002) *Developmental Coordination Disorder: Hints and Tips for the Activities of Daily Living*. London: Jessica Kingsley Publishers.

Case-Smith, J. (1994) "Self-care Strategies for Children with Developmental Deficits." In C. Christansen (ed.) *Ways of Living: Self-Care Strategies for Special Needs* (pp.101–156) Rockville, MD: American Occupational Therapy Association.

Ernsperger, L. and Stegen-Hanson, T. (2004) *Just Take a Bite: Easy, Effective Answers to Food Aversions and Eating Challenges*. Austin, TX: Future Horizons.

McClannahan, L.E. and Krantz, P.J. (1998) *Activity Schedules for Children with Autism: Teaching Independent Behavior*. Bethesda, MD: Woodbine House.

Wheeler, M. (1998) *Toilet Training for Individuals with Autism and Related Disorders*. Austin, TX: Future Horizons.

Sensory integration therapy

American Occupational Therapy Association (2003) "Applying sensory integration framework in educationally related occupational therapy practice." *American Journal of Occupational Therapy 57*, 652–659.

* Ayres, A.J. (1979) *Sensory Integration and the Child*. Los Angeles, CA: Western Psychological Services.

* Biele, L. and Peske, N. (2005) *Raising a Sensory Smart Child*. New York: Penguin Books.

Bundy, A.C., Lane, S.J. and Murray, E.A. (eds) (2002) *Sensory Integration Theory and Practice, Second Edition*. Philadelphia, PA: F.A. Davis.

Hoen, T.P. and Baumeister, A.A. (1994) "A critique of the application of sensory integration therapy to children with learning disabilities." *Journal of Learning Disabilities 27*, 6, 338–350.

Humphries, T.W., Snider, L. and McDougal, B. (1993) "Clinical evaluation of the effectiveness of sensory integrative and perceptual motor therapy in improving sensory integrative function in children with learning disabilities." *Occupational Therapy Journal of Research 13*, 3, 163–182.

* Kranowitz, C.S. (2006) *The Out-of-Sync Child: Recognizing and Coping with Sensory Integration Dysfunction, Revised Edition*. New York, NY: Perigee Trade.

Law, M., Polatajko, H.J., Miller, J., Schaffer, R. and Macnab, J. (1991) "The impact of heterogeneity in a clinical trial: Motor outcomes after sensory integrative therapy." *Occupational Therapy Journal of Research 11*, 3, 177–189.

* Miller, L.J. (2006) *Sensational Kids: Hope and Help for Children with Sensory Processing Disorders*. New York: Putnam Adult.

Polatajko, H.J., Law, M., Miller, J., Schaffer, R. and Macnab, J. (1991) "The effect of a sensory integration program on academic achievement, motor performance, and self-esteem in children identified as learning disabled: Results of a clinical trial." *Occupational Therapy Journal of Research 11*, 3, 155–176.

Schaaf, R.C. and Miller, L.J. (2005) "Occupational therapy using a sensory integrative approach for children with developmental disabilities." *Mental Retardation and Developmental Disabilities Research Reviews 11*, 2, 143–148.

* Smith, K.A. and Gouze, K.R. (2004) *The Sensory-Sensitive Child: Practical Solutions for Out-of-Bounds Behavior*. New York: Collins Publishers.

Social skills development

Chen, H. and Cohn, E.S. (2003) "Social participation for children with developmental coordination disorder: Conceptual, evaluation, and intervention considerations." *Physical and Occupational Therapy in Pediatrics 23*, 4, 61–78.

* Freedman, J.S. (2002) *Easing the Teasing: Helping Your Child Cope with Name-Calling, Ridicule, and Verbal Bullying*. New York, NY: McGraw-Hill.

Gutstein, S.E. and Sheely, R.K. (2002) *Relationship Development Intervention with Young Children: Social and Emotional Development Activities for Asperger Syndrome, Autism, PDD, and NLD*. London: Jessica Kingsley Publishers.

Mannix, D. (1993) *Social Skills Activities for Special Children*. West Nyack, NY: The Center for Applied Research in Education.

* Nowicki, S. and Duke, M.P. (1992) *Helping the Child Who Doesn't Fit In*. Atlanta, GA: Peachtree Publishers.

* Osman, B.B. and Blinder, H. (1989) *No One to Play With: The Social Side of Learning Disabilities*. Novato, CA: Academic Therapy Publications.

Rigby, K. (2002) *Stop the Bullying: A Handbook for Schools*. London: Jessica Kingsley Publishers.

* Thompson, M. and Cohen, L.J. (2002) *Mom, They're Teasing Me: Helping Your Child Solve Social Problems*. New York: Ballantine Books.

Williamson, G.G. (1993) "Enhancing the social competence of children with learning disabilities." *Sensory Integration Special Interest Section Newsletter 16*, 1, 1–2.

Zeitlin, S. and Williamson, G.G. (1994) *Coping in Young Children: Early Intervention Practices to Enhance Adaptive Behavior and Resilience*. Baltimore, MD: Paul H. Brookes.

Speech apraxia and oral-motor problems

*Agin, M., Geng, L. and Nicholl, M.J. (2003) *The Late Talker: What to Do if Your Child Isn't Talking Yet*. New York: St. Martin's Press.

Hall, P.K., Jordan, L.S. and Robin, D.A. (2007) *Developmental Apraxia of Speech–Second Edition: Theory and Clinical Practice*. Austin, TX: Pro-Ed.

*Orr, C. (1998) *Mouth Madness: Oral Motor Activities for Children*. San Antonio, TX: Therapy Skill Builders.

Silverman, F.L. and Kolody-Cost, M.C. (2004) *Let's Get Ready! A Developmental Motor Skills Program for Speech and OT*. East Moline, Il: Linguisystems.

Velleman, S.L. (2003) *Childhood Apraxia of Speech Resource Guide*. Clifton Park, NY: Delmar Learning.

Vision and perception

Gentile, M. (2005) *Functional Vision Behavior in Children: An Occupational Therapy Guide to Evaluation and Treatment Options*. Bethesda, MD: AOTA Press.

* Hickman, L. and Hutchins, R. (2002) *Seeing Clearly: Fun Activities for Improving Visual Skills*. Las Vegas, NV: Sensory Resources.

* Kurtz, L.A. (2006) *Visual Perception Problems in Children with ADHD, Autism, and Other Learning Disabilities: A Guide for Parents and Professionals*. London: Jessica Kingsley Publishers.

Scheiman, M. (2002) *Understanding and Managing Vision Deficits: A Guide for Occupational Therapists, Second Edition*. Thorofare, NJ: Slack, Inc.

Appendix III

HELPFUL AGENCIES AND ORGANIZATIONS

Ability.org
16 Almond Close
Penwortham, Preston PR1 0YQ, UK
www.ability.org.uk
Website offering an extensive listing of links to disability-related topics.

ADHD UK Alliance
209–211 City Road
London EC1V 1JN, UK
Tel: +44 (0)20 7608 8760
www.adhdalliance.org.uk
This organization is devoted to raising awareness, influencing policy, and improving services for children and others affected by ADHD.

Administration for Children and Families
US Department of Health and Human Services
Mail Stop HHH 300–F
370 L'Enfant Promenade, SW
Washington, DC 20447
www.acf.hhs.gov/programs/add
Provides information and referrals to federally funded agencies and organizations that provide services to persons with developmental disabilities.

All About Vision Consumer Guide
www.allaboutvision.com
This website offers an extensive consumer guide on subjects relating to eye health, vision care, and learning disabilities.

American Academy of Pediatrics
141 Northwest Point Boulevard
Elk Grove Village, IL 60007
Tel: +1 (847) 434-4000
www.aap.org
Organization that offers general information about children from birth through age 21, including research reports, policy, and technical reports on a wide range of subjects pertaining to child health.

American Association on Intellectual and Developmental Activities (AAIDD)
444 North Capitol Street NW, Suite 846
Washington, DC 20001-1512
Tel: +1 (202) 387-1968, +1 (800) 424-3688
www.aamr.org
This organization promotes progressive policies, sound research, effective practices, and universal human rights for people with intellectual and developmental disabilities.

American Occupational Therapy Association, Inc.
4720 Montgomery Lane
P.O. Box 31220
Bethesda, MD 20824-1220
Tel: +1 (301) 652-2682
www.aota.org
Professional membership organization of occupational therapists. Provides public education and referrals for occupational therapy services.

American Physical Therapy Association
1111 N. Fairfax Street
Alexandria, VA 22314-1489
Tel: +1 (800) 999-2782
www.apta.org
Professional membership organization of physical therapists. Operates clearinghouse for questions on physical therapy and disabilities.

American Psychological Association (APA)
750 First Street NE
Washington, DC 20002-4242
Tel: +1 (800) 374-2721, +1 (202) 336-6123 (Telecommunication device for the deaf
(TDD)/teletypewriter (TTY))
www.apa.org
This scientific and professional organization represents psychology in the United
States.

American Speech-Language Association (ASHA)
10801 Rockville Pike
Rockville, MD 20852
Tel: +1 (800) 638-8255
www.asha.org
This is the professional, scientific, and credentialing association for members and
affiliates who are speech-language pathologists, audiologists, and speech, language
and hearing scientists in the United States.

Association of University Centers on Disability (AUCD)
1010 Wayne Avenue, Suite 920
Silver Spring, MD 20910
Tel: +1 (301) 588-8252
www.aucd.org
This association provides access to regional University Affiliates Programs which
offer assessment, treatment, advocacy and referral services for children with
neurodevelopmental disabilities.

Autism Independent UK
www.autismuk.com
This useful website offers many information resources for parents and professionals, including extensive links to worldwide websites relating to autism.

Autism Society of America
7910 Woodmont Avenue, Suite 300
Bethesda, MD 20814-3067
www.autism-society.org
This agency provides a range of information and referral services for children with
autism.

The Bobath Centre
Bradbury House
250 East End Road
East Finchley, London N2 8AU, UK
Tel: +44 (0)20 8444 3355
www.bobath.org.uk
A registered charity devoted to treatment of children and adults through neurodevelopmental therapy. Offers a range of information for parents and adults, including workshops and certifications in neurodevelopmental therapy — the Bobath approach.

British Association/College of Occupational Therapists
106–114 Borough High Street
Southwark, London SE1 1LB, UK
Tel: +44 (0)20 7357 6480
www.baot.co.uk
The professional and trade union body for occupational therapy in the United Kingdom.

British Psychological Society
St. Andrews House
48 Princess Road East
Leicester LE1 7DR, UK
Tel: +44 (0)116 254 9568
www.bps.org.uk
This is the representative body for psychology and psychologists in the United Kingdom.

CHADD National
8181 Professional Place, Suite 150
Landover, MD 20785
Tel: +1 (301) 306-7070, +1 (800) 233-4050 (National Resource Center on ADHD)
www.chadd.org
Sponsors support groups for parents of children with attention deficit hyperactivity disorders. Provides continuing education programs for parents and professionals.

Chartered Society of Physiotherapy
14 Bedford Row
London WC1R 4ED, UK
Tel: +44(0) 20 7306 6666
www.csp.org.uk
This is the professional, educational and trade union body for physiotherapists in the United Kingdom.

Cherab Foundation
P.O. Box 8534 PSL
Florida 34952-8524
Tel: +1 (772) 335-5135
www.cherab.org
Organization devoted to education and research related to verbal apraxia and other childhood communication disorders.

Childhood Apraxia of Speech Association of North America (CASANA)
1151 Freeport Road #243
Pittsburgh, PA 15238
www.apraxia-kids.org
Organization that offers comprehensive information pertaining to childhood apraxia of speech and other speech and language topics.

Children's Defense Fund
25 E Street NW
Washington, DC 20001
Tel: +1 (202) 628-8787
www.childrensdefense.org
Provides information about legislation pertaining to child health, welfare, and education. Publishes a guide describing rights under the Individuals with Disabilities Education Act.

Children's Vision Information Network
www.childrensvision.com
This is a useful website that offers excellent reviews of the relationship of vision to learning.

College of Optometrists in Vision Development
243 N. Lindbergh Boulevard, Suite 310
St. Louis, MO 63141
Tel: +1 (888) 268-3770
www.covd.org
This website offers extensive resource information about the role of vision in autism, ADHD, and learning disabilities, as well as a directory of qualified optometrists.

Developmental Delay Resources
4401 East-West Highway, Suite 207
Bethesda, MD 20814
Tel: +1 (301) 653-2263
www.devdelay.org
This organization serves as a clearinghouse on alternative approaches to educational and medical treatment for children with special needs.

The Dyspraxia Foundation
8 West Alley, Hitchin
Hertfordshire SG5 1EG, UK
Tel: +44 (0)1462 454 986
www.dyspraxiafoundation.org.uk
A charitable organization dedicated to increasing awareness of dyspraxia.

Educational Resources Information Center (ERIC)
ERIC Clearinghouse on Disabilities and Gifted Education
Council for Exceptional Children
1110 North Glebe Road, Suite 300
Arlington, VA 22201
Tel: +1 (888) 232-7733, +1 (866) 915-5000 (TTY)
www.ericec.org
Association for parents and professionals with an interest in children with developmental differences. Provides literature reviews, referrals, and computer searches.

Future Horizons, Inc.
71 West Abram Street
Arlington, TX 76013
Tel: +1 (800) 489-0727
www.futurehorizons-autism.com
This organization offers publications and continuing education opportunities relating to autism. It also offers useful links to other autism-related websites.

Institute for Complementary Medicine
P.O. Box 194
London SE16 7QZ, UK
Tel: +44 (0)20 7237 5265
www.i-c-m.org.uk
A registered charity that provides public information on all aspects of safe and best practices of complementary medicine.

Learning Disabilities Association of America (LDA)
4156 Library Road
Pittsburgh, PA 15234-1349
Tel: +1 (412) 341-1515
www.ldanatl.org
Disseminates information, provides advocacy, and seeks to improve education opportunities for individuals with learning disabilities.

Learning Disabilities Online
www.ldonline.org
This website is a national educational service of WETA-TV, the Public Broadcast station in Washington, DC. It offers extensive information and resources relating to learning disabilities and ADHD.

Myomancy Foundation
www.myomancy.com
A comprehensive database of articles relating to treatments available for autism, ADHD, and learning disabilities.

National Autistic Society
393 City Road
London EC1V 1NG, UK
Tel: +44 (0)20 7833 2299
www.nas.org.uk
This organization offers resources and services for children with autism and their
families residing in the United Kingdom.

National Center for Complementary and Alternative Medicine
P.O. Box 7923
Gaithersburg, MD 20898-7923
Tel: +1 (888) 644-6226 (US), (301) 519-3153 (International),
+1 (866) 464-3615 (TTY)
www.nccam.nih.gov

National Center for Learning Disabilities
381 Park Avenue South, Suite 1401
New York, NY 10016
Tel: +1 (888) 575-7373
www.ncld.org
Promotes public awareness of learning disabilities by publishing a magazine
for parents and professionals, and providing computer-based information and
referral services.

National Education Association (NEA)
1201 16th Street NW
Washington, DC 20036-3290
Tel: +1 (202) 883-4000
www.nea.org
This professional employee organization is committed to advancing the cause of
public education in the United States, and offers a variety of resources to parents
and professionals.

**National Information Center for Children and Youth with Disabilities
(NICCHY)**
P.O. Box 1492
Washington, DC 20013
Tel: +1 (800) 695-0285 (TTY)
www.nichcy.org
Federal agency that provides referrals, information packages, and publications to
parents and family members.

Neuro-Developmental Treatment Association (NDTA)
1540 S. Coast Highway, Suite 203
Laguna Beach, CA 92651
Tel: +1 (800) 869-9295
www.ndta.org
Provides training and information about neurodevelopmental treatment. Provides a directory of therapists who are certified in neurodevelopmental therapy techniques.

Optometric Extension Program
1921 E. Carnegie Avenue, Suite 3-L
Santa Ana, CA 92705-5510
Tel: +1 (949) 250-8070
www.oep.org
This agency offers extensive articles and resources for parents and professionals, as well as an online store for books relating to vision and disabilities.

The Royal College of Speech and Language Therapists
2 White Hart Yard
London SE1 1NX, UK
Tel: +44 (0)20 7378 1200
www.rcslt.org
This is the professional body for speech and language therapists and support workers in the United Kingdom.

Sensory Integration International (SII)
P.O. Box 5339
Torrance, CA 90510-5339
Tel: +1 (301) 787-8805
www.sensoryint.com
A nonprofit organization devoted to developing awareness, knowledge, skills, and services in sensory integration. Provides advanced continuing education programs for therapists interested in sensory integration, including certification in the *Sensory Integration and Praxis Tests (SIPT)*. Publishes a directory of occupational and physical therapists who have been certified in the SIPT.

Special Abilities Ltd.
P.O. Box 360
Wakefield WF2 8QR, UK
Tel: +44 (0)1924 385977
www.abilities.fsnet.co.uk
Offers information, advice and support for parents of children with disabilities.

Zero to Three
National Center for Infants, Toddlers and Families
2000 M Street, NW, Suite 200
Washington, DC 20036
Tel: +1 (202) 638-1144, +1 (800) 899-4301
www.zerotothree.org
Organization geared towards helping parents and professionals support the physical, cognitive, and social-emotional growth of children of ages zero to three. Publishes the magazine, *Zero to Three*.

Appendix IV

SUPPLIERS OF TOYS, TESTS, AND OTHER EDUCATIONAL MATERIALS

Abilitations
3155 Northwoods Parkway
Norcross, GA 30071
Tel: +1 (800) 850-8602 (US), +1 (770) 449-5700 (International)
www.abilitations com

Academic Therapy Publications
20 Commercial Boulevard
Novato, CA 94949-6191
Tel: +1 (800) 422-7249 (US), +1 (415) 883-3314 (International)
www.AcademicTherapy.com

AGS Publishing/Pearson Assessment
P.O. Box 1416
Minneapolis, MN 55440
Tel: +1 (800) 627-7271
www.pearsonassessments.com

Brightminds
WellsWay Works
Wells Road, Radstock, Bath BA3 3RZ, UK
Tel: +44 (0)870 4422 144
www.brightminds.co.uk

Childcraft Education Corporation
P.O. Box 3239
Lancaster, PA 17604
Tel: +1 (800) 631-5652
www.childcraft.com

Creative Therapy Store
12031 Wilshire Boulevard
Los Angeles, CA 90025-1251
Tel: +1 (800) 648-8857
www.creativetherapystore.com

Flaghouse, Inc.
601 Flaghouse Drive
Hasbruck Heights, NJ 07604-3116
Tel: +1 (800) 793-7900 or +1 (201) 288-7600 (US), +1 (800) 265-6900 or
+1 (416) 495-8262 (Canada)
www.flaghouse.com

Funtastic Learning
5714 W. Gulf Bank
Rd. # 175
Houston, TX 77088
Tel: +1 (800) 314-7142
www.funtasticlearningtoys.com

Handwriting Without Tears/The Print Tool
8001 MacArthur Boulevard
Cabin John, MD 20818
Tel: +1 (301) 263-2700
www.hwtears.com

Harcourt Assessment (England)
1 Proctor Street
London WC1V 6EU, UK
Tel: +44 (0)20 7911 1975
www.harcourt-uk.com

Harcourt Assessment Inc.
19500 Bulverde Road
San Antonio, TX 78259-3701
Tel: +1 (800) 211-8378
www.harcourtassessment.com

Linguisystems
3100 4th Avenue
East Moline, IL 61244
Tel: +1 (800) 776-4332
www.linguisystems.com

OT Ideas, Inc.
124 Morris Turnpike
Randolph, NJ 07869
Tel: +1 (877) 768-4322, +1 (973) 895-3622
www.otideas.com

OT Ideas, Inc. (Canada)
P.O. Box 56091
Stony Creek, Ontario L8G5C9
Tel: +1 (877) 768-4332

PDP Products
14524 61st Street Ct. No
Stillwater, MN 55082
Tel: +1 (651) 439-8865
www.pdppro.com

Pocket Full of Therapy
P.O. Box 174
Morganville, NJ 07751
Tel: +1 (732) 441-0404, +1 (800) pfot-124
www.pfot.com

Pro-Ed
8700 Shoal Creek Boulevard
Austin, TX 78757-6897
Tel: +1 (800) 897-3202
www.proedinc.com

PsychCorp/Harcourt Assessment, Inc.
19500 Bulverde Road
San Antonio, TX 78259-3701
Tel: +1 (800) 872-1726
www.psychcorp.com

Psychological and Educational Publications, Inc.
P.O. Box 520
Hydesville, CA 95547-0520
Tel: +1 (800) 523-5775
www.psych-edpublications.com

Riverside Publishing Company
425 Spring Lake Drive
Itasca, IL 60143-2079
Tel: +1 (800) 323-9540 (US), +1 (630) 467-7000 (International)
www.riverpub.com

SenseToys
13 Barnsbury Terrace
London N1 1JH, UK
Tel: +44 (0)845 257 0849
www.sensetoys.com

Sensory Comfort Catalog
P.O. Box 6589
Portsmouth, NH 03802-6589
Tel: +1 (888) 436-8422
www.sensorycomfort.com

The Sensory Company International Ltd.
Broad Lane Business Centre
Westfield Lane
South Elmsall WF9 2JX, UK
Tel: +44 (0)845 838 2233
www.thesensorycompany.co.uk

Smart Start Toys
64 Palesgate Lane
Crowborough, East Sussex, TN6 3HF, UK
Tel: +44 (0)1892 65932
www.smartstart-toys.co.uk

Southpaw Enterprises
P.O. Box 1047
Dayton, OH 45401
Tel: +1 (800) 228-1698 (US), +1 (907) 252-7676 (International)
www.southpawenterprises.com

Sportime Abilitations
1 Sportime Way
Atlanta, GA 30340
Tel: +1 (800) 850-8602
www.abilitations.com

Texas Scottish Rite Hospital
2222 Welborn Street
Dallas, TX 75219
Tel: +1 (800) 421-1121

TFH Special Needs Toys — UK
5–7 Severnside Business Park
Severn Road, Stourport-on-Severn
Worcestershire, DY13 9HT, UK
Tel: +44 (0)1299 827820
www.tfhuk.com

TFH Special Needs Toys — USA
4537 Gibsonia Road
Gibsonia, PA 15044
Tel: +1 (800) 467-6222
www.tfhusa.com

Therapro, Inc.
225 Arlington Street
Framingham, MA 01702-8723
Tel: +1 (800) 257-5376, +1 (508) 872-9494
www.theraproducts.com

Therapy Shoppe, Inc.
P.O. Box 8875
Grand Rapids, MI 49508
Tel: +1 (800) 261-5590
www.therapyshoppe.com

Toys to Grow On
2695 E. Dominguez St.
Carson, CA 90810
Tel: +1 (800) 987-4454
www.toystogrowon.com

Western Psychological Services
12031 Wilshire Boulevard
Los Angeles, CA 90025-1251
Tel: +1 (800) 648-8857
www.wpspublish.com

INDEX